FORGIVENESS

FORGIVENESS

Finding Freedom
through
Reconciliation

Avis Clendenen
and
Troy W. Martin

A Crossroad Book
The Crossroad Publishing Company
New York

The Crossroad Publishing Company
481 Eighth Avenue, New York, NY 10001

Copyright © 2002 by Avis Clendenen and Troy W. Martin

Printed in the United States of America

Library of Congress Cataloging-in-Publication Data

Clendenen, Avis.
    Forgiveness : finding freedom through reconciliation /
Avis Clendenen, Troy W. Martin.
        p.   cm.
    Includes bibliographical references.
    ISBN 0-8245-1964-7 (alk. paper)
        1. Forgiveness—Religious aspects—Catholic Church.   2.
Reconciliation—Religious aspects—Catholic Church.   I. Martin, Troy
W. II. Title
BV4647.F55 C57 2002
234'.5—dc21

                                                2001006498

    2   3   4   5   6   7   8   9   10   06   05   04   03   02

For
Susan and Pam
and

In memory of
Jude and Dan,
Who taught us much about forgiveness

❧

Contents

∽

Preface

❧

OVER FOUR YEARS AGO, we began sharing stories about our personal and ministerial experiences of the painful relational dilemmas that hold people emotionally and spiritually captive. Our experiences revealed that people were hurting from unhealed fractures in relationships. Betrayal and broken trust appeared as tragic inevitabilities in their human quest to love and be loved. Our continued conversations further revealed that people often experience painful fractures of love and trust in relationships of consequence and find themselves needing to engage the hard and hopeful personal and interpersonal work of facing into their broken relationships. Such is the common drama we all share and call life.

We became increasingly concerned that popular culture was skewing forgiveness into a purely individualistic process devoid of any interaction with those who offend. We became even more concerned about the enormous pressure placed on wounded persons to forgive even unrepentant and arrogant offenders in the name of Christian faith. As biblical and pastoral theologians, we sensed a responsibility to write about some dimensions of Christian faith that are useful for healing ruptures between persons who once experienced the flow of love and trust.

In this book, we depart from the popular culture and seek a different way—the way of working through the painful tangle of fractured relationships. We find that fractures in relationships of consequence are best resolved by interpersonally confronting the significant other who has harmed us. Investigating various approaches to confrontation, we discover that certain strategies are more conducive to a successful confrontation than others. Occasionally experiencing less than satisfying responses from those we confront, we discover that genuinely repentant responses facilitate the forgiveness exchange whereas other responses block this exchange. Even with our best efforts, however, some fractures refuse healing, and people have no viable choice except to entrust them and their significant others to the God of relationships. We are not always completely successful in resolving the painful fractures of love and trust in our relationships of consequence. However, through the experiences outlined in this book, we are better prepared now to address these fractures than when we first began this work.

We sympathetically offer this book to all people interested in healthy, satisfying relationships of consequence. It is written for those experiencing pain inflicted by a significant other. We hope it offers the reader some biblical, pastoral, and interpersonal insights on ways to engage a forgiveness that heals. The tangled web of human relationships, and especially broken ones, makes quick-fix, rigid how-to manuals ineffective. Furthermore, we hope the reader will adopt and adapt our recommendations to fit her or his own situation and find the book useful both for resolving painful relationships and for realizing satisfying, healthy relationships of consequence.

At the end of a long process, we gratefully recognize the important contributions others have made to our work along the way. We are especially indebted to all those whose life experiences are reflected in the three stories presented in these pages. We know their pain and promise will help others. Some readers may identify with the real-life emotions and struggles experienced by Cardinal Bernardin and Steven Cook as well as by the fictitious characters in the other stories.

We gratefully acknowledge the members of Theology South for initially recognizing the significance of our ideas in healing wounded relationships. We are indebted to our students from Saint Xavier University, Catholic Theological Union, and University of Saint Mary of the Lake/ Mundelein Seminary for testing our ideas through their own life experiences.

We are particularly indebted to Dr. Evelyn Eaton Whitehead, Dr. James Whitehead, and Sister Mary Brian Costello, R.S.M., whose careful reading and critique of our manuscript facilitated the depth of insight and clarity of practice we sought to express. We are also grateful to our conversation partners Judith Bobber and Sheryl Martin, whose constant interaction clarified our thoughts and sharpened the presentation of our ideas. We recognize the encouragement and assistance of our publishers

Dr. Gwendolin Herder, Paul McMahon, John Tintera, and Christine Phillips and extend our sincere gratitude to them.

Finally, we want to thank our siblings Laura Susan Etter and Pamela Renee Billings, who still engage in the relational drama of life, as well as Willliam Daniel Clendenen and Jude Anthony Clendenen, who now rest in the loving embrace of the God of relationships. To them we gratefully and lovingly dedicate this book.

AVIS CLENDENEN
TROY W. MARTIN

CHAPTER 1

Exploring the Dilemma of Fracture and Forgiveness through Story

❧

W HO HAS NOT EXPERIENCED an act of betrayal? Sadly, betrayal is part of the universal fabric of life. It is a simple statement of truth to say that every relationship involving love and trust creates the potential for serious interpersonal rupture. In the all-too-human ordinary and extraordinary events of life, who has not experienced the bewilderment and confusion that come from struggling to live through undeserved hurt? It is an ancient scriptural injunction that the sun ought not go down on one's anger toward another. Easier said than done. Authentic forgiveness is the hard and hopeful work of facing the hurt, revisiting the fractures in love and trust, experiencing the painful emotions, and walking the way of true Christian forgiveness. The forgiveness exchange is often not easy, but it is a necessary process for the restoration of personal well-being and the reclaiming of interpersonal relationships of consequence. In the early dawn of a new millennium, Christian believers are called to embrace the duty and daring of forgiveness.

> *The following pages present an understanding of Christian forgiveness that is biblically based, theologically sound, and practically helpful.*

The following pages present an understanding of Christian forgiveness that is biblically based, theologically sound, and practically helpful. The communal and interpersonal dimensions of the forgiveness exchange are based on the inherent mutuality between and among persons engaged in relationships of meaning and love. This exchange is not solely an intrapsychic release or transaction. The assumption that forgiveness can occur entirely through the manipulation of a person's internal feelings or attitudes alone is incomplete. The forgiveness exchange encourages people to stay with their pain and work toward the authentic human encounters that hold the possibility of true healing. The assumption that a person can do the work of forgiveness within the confines of his/her individual mind and heart diverts energy from the authentic mutuality of the healing process, masks the true depth of fractured relationships, and results in a pseudo forgiveness inconsistent with the forgiveness exchange expressed in the Christian Gospels. Consider the interpersonal and social dimensions of the following stories of fractured relationships in need of forgiveness.

THE SABOTAGED FORGIVENESS EXCHANGE

"I am going to hell," Marilyn reported to her pastoral counselor.

"Why do you say that," he asked.

"My pastor told me so," she responded.

"Why would your pastor say such a thing," queried her pastoral counselor.

Marilyn told her story. From age eight, a family member named Bill had repeatedly molested her and finally raped her when she became a teenager. Family gatherings terrified her because Bill was there and showed no remorse for his actions but continued to force himself upon her socially and physically. His arrogance especially offended her. Holidays were horror days for her as she sought to control the anger and bitterness she felt toward him. She was emotionally and physically exhausted at the end of such days from pretending to be enjoying herself and from seeking to avoid him.

As a religious person, Marilyn deeply wanted to forgive and forget the whole ugly experience. She prayed for God's help again and again, especially on occasions when she knew Bill would be present. She went through phases when she thought she had forgiven Bill and had even repressed the haunting memories. One encounter with him, however, proved she had not finished the process of forgiveness.

Figure 1
Forgiveness Exchange

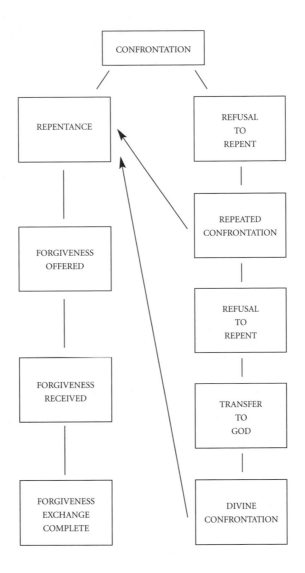

In her twenties, Bill tried to rape Marilyn again, but to their mutual surprise, an eruption of empowering anger enabled her to successfully resist. This incident triggered a greater depth of self-loathing and guilt as she wondered why he was so relentless toward her. Did she prompt it in him? Her confusion and bitterness deepened. Her depression manifested itself in self-destructive behaviors. She went through a series of unfulfilling relationships that left her with a child but no loving husband. Her bewildered mother, father, and siblings agonized over the "mess" of her life. She continued to sacrifice herself to maintain the silence of a belligerent peace.

Marilyn's pain simply grew too profound, and she finally conceded that she needed help. She longed to break the silence and be healed. She met with her pastor and told him the story. He listened and proceeded to inform her she must intensify her efforts to forgive and forget as the Bible teaches. He told her she must forgive Bill and proceeded to quote from the scripture: "But if you do not forgive others neither will your Father forgive your transgressions" (Matt. 6:15). She understood the implication. If she did not do the work of forgiving Bill, she would never receive the eternal reward of heaven.

> "But if you do not forgive others neither will your Father forgive your transgressions." (Matt. 6:15)

Marilyn became terrified because Bill's arrogance and impudence repeatedly sabotaged her most strenuous efforts to forgive. Time devoted to disciplined prayer and attempts to find it in her heart to forgive faltered in the face of his abusive attitudes and actions toward her. She simply could not forgive him and concluded that she was doomed to alienation from God into eternity. With firm conviction, therefore, she could say to her pastoral counselor, "My life is going to hell along with me."

How should this pastoral counselor advise Marilyn? Should he agree with her pastor and advise Marilyn to forgive and forget even when she finds it impossible to forgive? Is it healthy and moral for Marilyn to forgive Bill, who refuses to own the offense and to offer sorrow at the hurt he has caused her? What role should Marilyn and Bill's family play in assisting or arresting a potential confrontation and reconciliation? How can forgiveness be the answer to this fractured

Figure 2
Summary of the Forgiveness Exchange

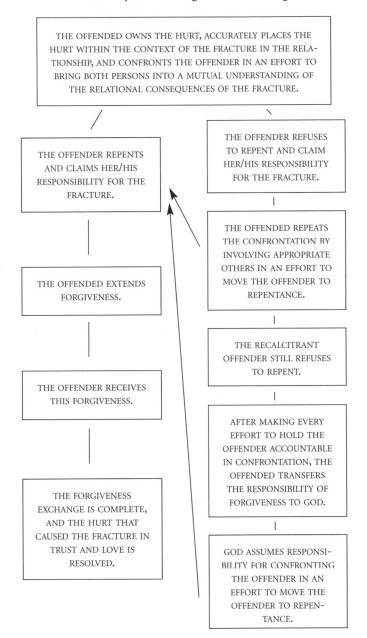

THE OFFENDED OWNS THE HURT, ACCURATELY PLACES THE HURT WITHIN THE CONTEXT OF THE FRACTURE IN THE RELATIONSHIP, AND CONFRONTS THE OFFENDER IN AN EFFORT TO BRING BOTH PERSONS INTO A MUTUAL UNDERSTANDING OF THE RELATIONAL CONSEQUENCES OF THE FRACTURE.

THE OFFENDER REPENTS AND CLAIMS HER/HIS RESPONSIBILITY FOR THE FRACTURE.

THE OFFENDER REFUSES TO REPENT AND CLAIM HER/HIS RESPONSIBILITY FOR THE FRACTURE.

THE OFFENDED EXTENDS FORGIVENESS.

THE OFFENDED REPEATS THE CONFRONTATION BY INVOLVING APPROPRIATE OTHERS IN AN EFFORT TO MOVE THE OFFENDER TO REPENTANCE.

THE OFFENDER RECEIVES THIS FORGIVENESS.

THE RECALCITRANT OFFENDER STILL REFUSES TO REPENT.

THE FORGIVENESS EXCHANGE IS COMPLETE, AND THE HURT THAT CAUSED THE FRACTURE IN TRUST AND LOVE IS RESOLVED.

AFTER MAKING EVERY EFFORT TO HOLD THE OFFENDER ACCOUNTABLE IN CONFRONTATION, THE OFFENDED TRANSFERS THE RESPONSIBILITY OF FORGIVENESS TO GOD.

GOD ASSUMES RESPONSIBILITY FOR CONFRONTING THE OFFENDER IN AN EFFORT TO MOVE THE OFFENDER TO REPENTANCE.

relationship when Bill's unrelenting arrogance sabotages the forgiveness exchange?

Marge, an eighty-year-old widow, lives alone in a middle-class urban neighborhood.[1] She has three married adult children who are successful professionals with families of their own. Since the death of Marge's husband over twenty-five years ago, her children have encouraged her to become more involved in life-giving activities. Marge has struggled with taking responsibility for her own needs and feels she deserves more attention from her children and grandchildren.

Following many years of frustrated efforts, Marge's children feel they have done all they can for their mother and continue to include her regularly in the activities of their families. They provide airline tickets so Marge can visit her eldest daughter Susan, who lives far away. Susan telephones her mother on a regular basis and spends time with her when she and her husband, Jack, are in town during holidays and the summer season. Jack has been attentive to his mother-in-law's needs ever since he married Susan over thirty years ago.

A single event triggered a devastating relational situation between Marge and her oldest daughter Susan. Susan and Jack approached Marge, who does not drive, about leaving a car Jack inherited in Marge's empty garage. Susan and Jack told Marge that they would then have a car while in town and would be able to do more things with and for her during the summer months. Susan's siblings have appreciated her and Jack's summertime availability, which relieves them of responsibility for Marge's doctor visits, shopping, and household needs. Marge was initially silent when Susan and Jack requested use of her empty garage. Then she questioned the safety of leaving the car in her garage. Susan pressed her mother to express how she really felt about their request. Marge responded that the whole idea made her very nervous and she simply did not want the responsibility.

Bewildered and angry, Jack left for fear of saying something he might later regret. Susan remained with her mother to make sure she understood what had just happened. Susan reminded her mother of their attention to her needs over the years and that they had never really asked her for anything before. The request seemed simple since the garage was empty. Susan could not grasp her mother's staunch resistance. In frustration, anger, and embarrassment at her mother's behavior toward her husband, Susan left her mother's house. Neither Susan nor Jack has returned or been invited to Marge's home in over four years.

> *In this unforgiving cycle, who could create a pressure point that would initiate a breakthrough?*

When queried by family members, Marge maintains that Jack and Susan owe her an apology, and she stubbornly refuses to engage them regarding the fractured relationship. This insignificant and seemingly benign event has deeply wounded the relationship between Marge and her daughter and son-in-law. Susan's siblings are troubled that such an insignificant incident caused such a significant problem. They are uncomfortable and saddened about the chasm of silence between and among family members over this unresolved rift. How can forgiveness disengage the relational paralysis and move this family toward a renewed sense of mutual love and authenticity when Marge's stubbornness appears to have stalled the forgiveness exchange?

In this unforgiving cycle, who could create a pressure point that would initiate a breakthrough? Should Susan confront her mother directly about the pain she, Jack, and their family experience? Can Susan first forgive her mother for her own sake before she verbally shares this fact with her mother? Do Susan's siblings have any further unexplored responsibility or opportunity to help in this stalled forgiveness exchange? In an effort to justify her decision to withhold the garage, has Marge stalemated needed authentic dialogue with her family? Because of Marge's history of "limited function," is she exempt from initiating action to heal the fracture in her relationships? Is there any role Marge can play in the healing of her family? What are the emotional and spiritual implications for this family as this stalled forgiveness exchange continues through the years?

THE SUCCESSFUL FORGIVENESS EXCHANGE

In the fall of 1993, a charge of sexual misconduct was leveled at the highest-ranking official of the Roman Catholic Church ever to be so accused; this accusation stunned the Catholic Church of Chicago, the church universal, and the world. Steven Cook, a former seminarian, accused Joseph Cardinal Bernardin, Archbishop of Chicago, and another priest of sexual abuse years ago in Cincinnati. Steven eventually left the seminary, struggled to come to terms with his homosexuality, and received treatment for emotional problems. He was living with and dying from AIDS at the time of his accusation.

Anyone who entered the presence of the cardinal during those agonizing months became aware of the humiliation, the terrible pain, and the cardinal's conviction that he would be vindicated. The stigma, however, was profound. Joseph Bernardin lived with the brutality of this dark cloud over his life for months. As the spring of 1994 emerged, Steven withdrew his charges against the cardinal because of his inability to remember with certainty that he had been abused by the then Bishop Bernardin. The cardinal was vindicated of all accusations of sexual misconduct. His good name was restored. Steven disappeared from news headlines; the story appeared to have ended.

> *"May this story give to anyone who is hurt or alienated the inspiration and courage to be reconciled."*

In January of 1995, the following headline appeared in newspapers across the country and around the world: "May this story give to anyone who is hurt or alienated the inspiration and courage to be reconciled." Cardinal Bernardin was back in the news and proclaimed that a further exchange was needed for authentic forgiveness and healing to take place between him and his accuser. Against the advice of close colleagues, Cardinal Bernardin wanted to face Steven in person, open again the wounds of his accusations, and search out the deeper and graced possibilities of the forgiveness exchange. The cardinal reported on his meeting and said, "I began by telling Steven that the only reason for requesting the meeting was to bring closure to the traumatic events of the last winter by personally letting him know that I harbored no ill feelings toward him and to pray with him for his physical and spiritual well being." Steven replied that he wanted to apologize in person for the embarrassment and hurt he had caused. "In other words," the cardinal wrote of this experience, "we both sought reconciliation."

The ensuing confrontation revealed a powerful vulnerability and mutuality between the offended and the offender. The cardinal and Steven gave witness to the reality that human beings do not heal by forgetting. Time alone does not heal; time only provides the context in which to do the healing. The cardinal made efforts to locate Steven, requested a meeting, traveled the distance from Chicago to Philadelphia, and spent two hours with Steven in the actual experience of the forgiveness exchange. Following the ritualizing of the exchange of forgiveness, the cardinal reflectively remarked, "Never in my forty-three years as a priest have I witnessed a more profound reconciliation. The words I am using to tell you this story cannot begin to describe the power of God's grace that was at work that afternoon. It was a manifestation of God's love, forgiveness, and healing that I will never forget."

> *Time alone does not heal; time only provides the context in which to do the healing.*

Since the cardinal had been fully vindicated, why did he need to confront Steven directly and seek mutual reconciliation? What mysterious or obvious process led to Joseph Bernardin's willingness to open wounds for the sake of deeper healing, a healing that he keenly felt needed to be experienced by both him and Steven? Can the forgiveness exchange be successful only among the highly skilled, the exceptionally holy, or the dying? Where do average people find the courage and compassionate skill to confront those who have hurt them? Where does a person find the absolute humility to own the power to seriously wound others and admit an intended or unintended offense? Christianity proclaims a forgiveness exchange. When successfully completed by the offended and offender, this exchange creates forces powerful enough to heal even the most wounded relationships as the mutual reconciliation of Steven Cook and Cardinal Bernardin demonstrates.

THE STORIES AND FINISHING UNFINISHED BUSINESS

The preceding stories reveal the sad and painful consequences of unfinished relational business and the power and possibility of heal-

ing the wounds between human beings. Whether intended or unintended, conscious or unconscious, behaviors that result in betrayal
and broken trust create situations that clamor for attention and
authentic healing. The stories of the sabotaged and the stalled forgiveness exchanges are essentially about the reality that unfinished
business will keep emerging, often uninvited, into the present until it
is adequately addressed.

The story of Cardinal Bernardin's successful forgiveness exchange
is an example of the possibility and the pathway of finishing unfinished business. Dr. Elisabeth Kübler-Ross deserves gratitude for developing this notion of unfinished business. According to Kübler-Ross,
unfinished business means that the best gift people give to themselves
and those they love is telling the truth about their emotions, their
anguish, their hate, their unresolved frustrations, their fears, and their
grief. Telling the truth about their emotions enables people to open
their hearts to healing and forgiveness so that they can be restored to
fullness of life without repression and guilt. People can finish unfinished business by learning to do their emotional and spiritual homework. The challenges described thus far may not be easily undertaken
by those with weakened mental competence, emotional instability, or
an underdeveloped moral sense. Nevertheless, relationship is a complex phenomenon in which there are varied kinds and degrees. Even
people quite debilitated can often meaningfully participate in relationships.

In the sabotaged forgiveness exchange, Marilyn's rape by a family
member is a traumatic and dramatic violation that has plagued her
life and shattered her sense of trust. The betrayal is so deep that it has
the power to plunge her, the victim, into self-doubt and self-recrimi-
nation when it is clear that evil has been perpetrated against her. She
is the victim of rape, which is always an undeserved act of interpersonal violence. Her inability to find the freedom to resolve this wound
has resulted in a sacrifice of herself for the sake of a silence that ultimately protects her offender. His apparent protection from the reality
of his offense is an unbearable and continuing experience of revictimization for Marilyn. He will not likely admit his responsibility,
especially in the absence of pressure to do so. By not being able to confront the truth openly, Marilyn's unfinished business with Bill deepens her pain and contributes to her enduring alienation within the
family.

The stalled forgiveness exchange is commonplace and appears on the surface to be a rather harmless event. Elderly Marge simply does not feel comfortable in occupying her empty garage with Susan and Jack's car. What appears neutral is really a watershed moment in the relationship between daughter, son-in-law, and mother. The confusion and anger that surround Marge's refusal of the request for use of the garage inaugurates a stalemate of silence that has existed for over four years. The free-flowing joys of family reunions around birthdays, weddings, and holidays have been shaded with a subtle fear that invades the whole family system. It has become clear to Marge's children that she is more willing to die in this condition than initiate attention to unfinished business. Her focus on the injustice done to her prevents her from reaching beyond her feelings. In a sense, she has become the offended offender.

> *Death—the physical absence of a person—does not end the unresolved or unattended conflicts between people and within families.*

Of course, the family is aware that Marge is in the end-time of her life. Death—the physical absence of a person—does not end the unresolved or unattended conflicts between people and within families. Unfortunately, these painful issues will not evaporate with Marge's death. Most likely, they will be "buried alive" and wait to emerge again, passed on to yet another generation. Silence and time do not heal. Silence and time provide the context in which to do the emotional and spiritual homework of preparing for the challenges of giving and receiving forgiveness. At the moment of forgiveness, the fruits of silence and time retreat before the courage that breaks silence and revisits betrayal in the graced and authentic human quest to restore trust and love and to live in a new time.

Cardinal Bernardin's successful forgiveness exchange illustrates that it is actually possible for the average person to make his or her way through the maze of interpersonal conflict and actually experience the exchange of giving and receiving forgiveness. Some say that coming face-to-face with the pain is simply more than what can be expected of people. American culture is particularly prone to promoting denial and avoidance and to reducing the power of repentance to explanation and excuses. The skill of blaming others and avoiding responsibility for relational situations results in the continuance of the cycle of broken trust and betrayal.

American Christian culture is rife with the dangerous trend of the acceptability, even expectation, of lying and fleeing from responsibility. Unfortunately, Christianity has allowed distorted messages to be communicated as biblical truth and has accepted mandates for Christian behavior that have not resulted in healthy and restored relationships, which are the "prize" of the forgiveness exchange. While it is true that forgiveness seeks reconciliation but does not require it, the position developed in the following pages is that the "final step" of striving for reconciliation remains a gospel imperative, an imperative that so touchingly compelled Cardinal Bernardin.

Bernardin demonstrated the extent to which one must go to travel the way of the authentic forgiveness exchange. He perceived the mutuality of the need for reconciliation. Even after forgiveness had been extended and received, he took the additional step of meeting face-to-face with his offender to confront the pain and celebrate new time with Steven Cook. Joseph and Steven evidence the possibility of successfully negotiating the scary and graced terrain of actually believing that persons can forgive and be healed of undeserved wounds, as well as be forgiven for inflicting such wounds and take responsibility for intended or unintended hurtful behavior. Most importantly, the successful forgiveness exchange demonstrated by the cardinal and Steven indicates that human beings can enter the experience of reconciliation that lasts into eternity.

APPLICATION

Such is the complexity of the human drama, the tangle of human relationships, and the everyday ordinary challenge of restoring the fragile bonds between human beings. As the text continues, you are invited to bring your own personal stories of fractured relationships into dialogue with the biblical, psychological, and theological understanding of the restoration of relationships. Consider using a journal/notebook to accompany you through the text as you begin to explore the contours of relational rupture and the challenges of facing into the dynamics of hurt and healing. Your journal is a private place for you to note important insights and to engage in the written exercises in the application section at the close of each chapter. Before proceeding to chapter 2, consider spending time with the following reflective exercises.

- ◆ Pause and reflect on the characters and human situations described in the three stories. With whom do you most identify? Marilyn or Bill in the sabotaged forgiveness exchange? Marge, Susan, or Jack in the stalled forgiveness exchange? Joseph or Steven in the successful forgiveness exchange? Someone else in each situation? With whom do you share an empathic identification? What memories, feelings, or insights does this prompt?

- ◆ With whom or with what situation do you feel uncomfortable, irritated, angry, or confused? Explore the reasons for the emergence of these difficult feelings or painful insights.

- ◆ In what ways do these characters and relational dilemmas remind you of similar persons and situations from your own life experience? Allow yourself sufficient time for your own story of betrayal and/or fracture in a relationship of consequence to crystallize and come into full consciousness. In the privacy of your journal, articulate your own story in a free-flow writing style and without any self-censure. Bring your own experience into direct dialogue with the reflective questions and relate the material in the book to your own life.

NOTES

1. This story is also the basis for a case study by Avis Clendenen, "Unfinished Business Among the Aging and Those Who Love Them," *Journal of Pastoral Care* 54, no. 2 (2000): 121–33.

CHAPTER 2

Interpersonal and Intrapsychic Models of Forgiveness

~

W HAT IS INTERPERSONAL FORGIVENESS? What distinguishes forgiveness from exoneration? Is forgiveness the same as reconciliation? Is the restoration of a broken relationship a by-product of forgiveness, or can one forgive or be forgiven without the reconciliation of the relationship? Can one engage in the forgiveness process without any interpersonal encounter with the one who inflicted the pain? Can forgiveness be achieved solely through intrapsychic processes? This chapter explores these probing and provocative questions.

Forgiveness that is humanly mature and Christian in nature is both a personal process and an interpersonal encounter whereby persons engage in the effort to face a fracture of trust and love to achieve a restoration of mutual well-being that is based in the experience of both justice and mercy. Forgiveness, then, is both a process and a decision to act. Interpersonal forgiveness is an event of Christian grace. The mysterious action of grace motivates and guides human desire to enter a process of healing. This process of healing will necessarily include the genuine effort of the offended and offender to come to terms with the meaning of a relational rupture in a relationship of consequence.

> *Forgiveness that is humanly mature and Christian in nature is both a personal process and an interpersonal encounter.*

14

In contrast to this understanding of Christian forgiveness, exoneration is a mature human gesture that exempts the offender from the interpersonal and social consequences that his or her act deserves. In attaining this emotional, spiritual, and relational gesture, the offended person comes to see the offender in the larger context of his or her life and is able through insight and understanding to accept that complex extenuating circumstances mitigate the offender's responsibility for the destructive impact of the offending behavior. Forgiveness is not required. Acceptance of the limitations of the wrongdoer exonerates the offender and frees the offended to decide to remain or not to remain in relationship with a nonculpable wrongdoer.

> *Forgiveness, however, differs from exoneration in that forgiveness requires some action from the person responsible for the fracture that originally caused the hurt.*

There are those within the emerging field of forgiveness studies who suggest that exoneration and forgiveness are intimately intertwined. The work of behavioral scientists and therapeutic practitioners Drs. Terry Hargrave and William T. Andersen build on the work of Ivan Boszormenyi-Nagy and suggest that exoneration is often a "station" in the movement toward forgiveness.[1] Exoneration helps the one injured understand the fallibility of the wrongdoer and stabilizes the position of the offended and offender in relation to each other.[2] Forgiveness, however, differs from exoneration in that forgiveness requires some action from the person responsible for the fracture that originally caused the hurt.

Reconciliation is about the mutual commitment to bring the personal experience of restored well-being back into the interpersonal context of a relationship. While forgiveness is required for reconciliation, complete reconciliation does not always follow from the successful forgiveness exchange. Reconciliation, like exoneration, is an intimate partner of forgiveness; yet forgiveness does not necessarily result in a fully restored relationship. Forgiveness may heal the depth of the emotional wounds, and yet the relationship may not move forward into a new time. In contrast, reconciliation is the restoration of interpersonal trust in the mutual commitment to invest again in the relationship. The partners in a reconciled relationship do not fear the memory of the fracture, harbor no unattended resentments, are willing to be vulnerable with each other again, and permit the relationship to be different than it was before. The reconciled relationship enters *new time*. The issue as to whether reconciliation precedes forgiveness or forgiveness precedes reconciliation is psychologically complex. What is clear theologically is that the movement in the direction of the desire to be freed from the pain of the wrongdoing and to enter a future not determined by the hurtful deed involves the Christian mystery of grace.

The *inter*personal dimension of the forgiveness-reconciliation process cannot be fully achieved solely by an individual within the confines of his or her own *intra*psychic processes. This means that forgiveness in its essence and fullness involves people and is therefore interpersonal. The idea that the whole of the forgiveness process can be accomplished solely within the context of a person's internal mind or psyche fails to value interpersonal engagement in addressing the hurt. The notion that the offender has no obligations to the offended or that the offended can sufficiently heal without any effort at encounter with the offender removes the process of Christian forgiveness from its communal/social context and fails to meet the standards of forgiveness suggested by the Christian Gospel.

> *The interpersonal dimension of the forgiveness-reconciliation process cannot be fully achieved solely by an individual within the confines of his or her own intrapsychic processes.*

Forgiveness is a social experience that must involve both engagement and exchange between the offended and the offender, the injured and the wrongdoer. The forgiveness exchange is facilitated by the offended's confronting the offender and the offender's repenting from her or his part in the brokenness. If either confrontation—facing the hurt—or repentance—owning the hurt—is absent, the forgiveness exchange cannot take place. In a failed forgiveness exchange, the offended may need to transfer the responsibility of forgiving to God and recognize that the forgiveness exchange may not be possible at the present time. The forgiveness exchange enables a restoration process to begin that, over time, brings the offended and the offender into authentic relationship, a relationship experienced in new time.

THE EMERGENCE OF THE *INTRA*PSYCHIC MODEL

Since the 1980s, numerous researchers and practitioners in such diverse fields as psychology, psychiatry, medicine, theology, philosophy, social work, counseling, and education have expressed an increasing interest in the issue of forgiveness. Dr. Robert Enright, an educational psychologist, has focused this interest by founding the International Forgiveness Institute to provide an interdisciplinary forum for researching and discussing the topic of forgiveness. Participants in this institute study the processes of forgiveness in a multidisciplinary manner and have produced several works that reflect the developmental and psychological assumptions of this institute.[3] The definition and model of forgiveness developed by this institute are gaining an increasing acceptance not only in the secular but also in the religious sectors of contemporary culture.

The definition and model of forgiveness developed by this institute frequently find their way into Christian thought and practice. Before the understanding of forgiveness advocated by this institute receives Christian acceptance, however, it should be compared to the understanding of forgiveness presented in the Christian scriptures and theological reflection, as well as in Christian liturgical and sacramental practice. Such a comparison offers a significant critique of the institute's notion of forgiveness relative to the interpersonal understanding of forgiveness in Christian thought and practice.

Even though the institute consistently claims that its understanding of forgiveness is *inter*personal, this claim requires some important qualifications. According to Enright and his colleagues, "interpersonal forgiveness" is between people and only occurs between people. Since forgiveness is always occasioned by one person's hurting or injuring another, they claim that their understanding of forgiveness is interpersonal. Beyond the interpersonal situation that occasions the need for forgiveness, however, "between people" does not seem to mean interpersonal engagement. Their definition and model do not require a face-to-face encounter or even communication and interaction

between the offended and the offender as Matthew 18 recommends
and as Joseph Bernardin demonstrates in his encounter with Steven
Cook. Instead of advocating interpersonal engagement, Enright and
his associates situate the process of forgiveness solely within the cog-
nitive and emotional processes of the offended. In spite of their claim,
intrapsychic rather than *interpersonal* is a far more appropriate desig-
nation of their understanding of forgiveness.

The intrapsychic understanding of forgiveness is evident in the
institute's definition of forgiveness, which reads as follows:

> Forgiveness is the overcoming of negative affect and judgment toward
> the offender, not by denying ourselves the right to such affect and judg-
> ment, but by endeavoring to view the offender with compassion,
> benevolence, and love while recognizing that he or she has abandoned
> the right to them.[4]

According to this definition, the offended forgives by "overcoming
negative affect and judgment toward the offender." The injured
achieves this mental and emotional state by viewing "the offender
with compassion, benevolence, and love" even though the offender
has forfeited any claim to these attitudes. By mentioning both
offender and offended, this definition appears to be interpersonal.
However, the offender does not play an active role and is merely a passive recipient of the offended's emotions and mental perceptions. The
entire process takes place in the mind and heart of the injured, and the
offender may even be oblivious to the entire process. Since this definition does not require interpersonal engagement and contains forgiveness within the mental and emotional activity of the injured, this
definition presents an intrapsychic rather than an interpersonal understanding of forgiveness.

The intrapsychic dimension of the institute's approach to forgiveness is further demonstrated by the four phases in the institute's
model of forgiveness.[5] During the first or "Uncovering Phase," the
offended "becomes aware of the emotional pain that has resulted from
a deep, unjust injury." The offended must process this pain and not
only confront but also understand the negative emotions such as
anger and hatred that arise from the pain. Healing only begins when
the offended brings these and other painful emotions "out into the
open." In the second or "Decision Phase," the injured "realizes that to
continue to focus on the injury and on the injurer may cause more

unnecessary suffering" and "commits to forgiving the injurer who has caused her or him such pain." This decision leads to the third or "Work Phase," in which the offended strives "to understand the life context of the offender and to see a possible reason for causing such hurt." The offended works to feel empathy for the offender by recognizing him or her as a limited fellow human being. The offended accepts the pain "that resulted from the actions of the injurer" and "chooses not to pass it on to others, including the offender." During the final phase, or "Outcome/Deepening Phase," the injured person gains "emotional relief from the process of forgiving the injurer" and experiences inner healing and the resultant freedom. The emphasis on altering the offended's inner mental and emotional states in each phase demonstrates the intrapsychic dimension of the institute's approach to forgiveness. These intrapsychic processes reveal an emotional artistry that abides within human capacity. The researchers and practitioners of the institute have made a significant contribution in so clearly surveying and expressing the dynamics of the inner emotional life of human beings.

In each of these phases, however, the entire forgiveness process requires the inner emotional homework of the offended without involvement or engagement with the offender. The one offended must recognize that the offense is unjust, realize the need to be released from negative affect toward the offender, work toward a change of heart by contextualizing the offender's deed, abandon feelings of revenge, and restore a sense of positive regard and optimism toward the humanity of the offender. The obligation for initiating, continuing, and completing the process rests solely upon the offended. This is a heavy load for one party in a relationship to bear. The offender has no obligations, no invitations, and need not even apologize to facilitate the forgiveness process since the injured party's healing does not rely on the offender's consciousness of her or his hurtful actions or inaction or upon the offender's regret. For Enright and his colleagues,

> *In spite of their claim, intrapsychic rather than interpersonal is a far more appropriate designation of their understanding of forgiveness.*

"forgiveness is the self-sacrificial gift of love" and "a gift given need not await a prior response from the other person."[6] Releasing the offender from obligation while requiring self-sacrifice from the offended suggests an experience of forgiveness that may unintentionally, yet inevitably revictimize the injured person.

Even though the institute claims that its understanding of forgiveness is interpersonal, its understanding of forgiveness as a series of intrapsychic transactions fails to fully embrace and articulate the interpersonal dimension of forgiveness expressed in Christian scriptures, tradition, and theological reflection. According to the institute, the individual who has been hurt proceeds through the various phases without any expectation for the wrongdoer to enter at any point in this process. The one wounded is expected to do sufficient inner work to reach a point where she or he can extend forgiveness to the wrongdoer as an act of moral love. Processes that are purely internal to the individual may indeed result in an inner sense of freedom and serenity, and such inner healing is no small feat. The assumption that forgiveness can occur through inner actions and transactions within one's internal feelings and attitudes alone, however, ignores the social dimensions in which forgiveness occurs within the Christian community. The Christian understanding of forgiveness not only provides for the grace of intrapsychic healing but also allows for the grace of interpersonal healing.

APPLICATION

Christian scholars, ministers, and pastoral counselors among others will benefit from the following chapters, which investigate interpersonal forgiveness through a Christian lens. Such biblical, theological, and pastoral perspectives offer alternatives to the intrapsychic forgiveness gaining national attention through the efforts of the International Forgiveness Institute.

The *intrapsychic* approach to forgiveness means that the one offended engages in a series of emotional and mental processes to come to terms with the hurt by overcoming "any negative affect or judgments toward the offender." Forgiveness in this model is a "self-sacrificial gift of love and need not wait for or expect a response from the offender."

The *interpersonal* approach to forgiveness means that one party in the fractured relationship (usually the one who experiences the hurt) will, at the appropriate time, attempt a direct encounter with the offender in order to face into the hurt together for the hope of experiencing authentic repentance, shared forgiveness, and the restoration of mutual well-being.

In short, the *intrapsychic* approach permits the whole of the forgiveness process to be contained within the inner mental and emotional dynamics of the offended person and does not require any involvement of the one who offended. The *interpersonal* approach suggests that the process of healing must include the genuine effort of the offended and offender to come to terms with the meaning of the relational rupture in a relationship of consequence, except in cases where direct encounter would be emotionally or physically dangerous.

Exoneration exempts the offender from the consequences of his or her behavior due to extenuating circumstances that mitigate the offender's responsibility for the destructive impact of the offending behavior.

- ♦ Reflecting on the descriptions and distinctions offered above, with which approach do you resonate? Which approach best describes your way of handling serious breaks in your relationships of consequence?

- ♦ Complete the following "unfinished sentences" with the first "unfiltered" response that surfaces for you:

  - ➤ I remember successfully using the *intrapsychic* approach to forgiveness in healing a significant rift in relationship with . . .

  - ➤ Following my internal offer of forgiveness to the offender, my relationship with her/him . . .

  - ➤ In that instance, my internal effort was rewarded by the offender . . .

  - ➤ The prospect of actually preparing to directly face a person who has wounded me makes me . . .

  - ➤ The time I confronted an offender and appropriately faced him or her with the impact of the wounding behavior resulted in . . .

  - ➤ In this instance, my effort to face a person with whom I previously experienced love and trust was rewarded by . . .

➤ After considering more careful distinctions between forgiveness and exoneration, I am aware that I exonerated _____
because . . .

➤ In this instance, the exonerated relationship . . .

➤ The working definition of forgiveness that makes most sense
to me is . . .

NOTES

1. Ivan Boszormenyi-Nagi is one of the founders of the family therapy movement in the United States and a pioneer theorist in contextual therapy. See Terry Hargrave, *Families and Forgiveness: Healing Wounds in the Intergenerational Family* (New York: Brunner/Mazel, 1997), 45–48. For a detailed understanding of the ledger/entitlement model of family relationships, see I. Boszormenyi-Nagi and B. Krasner, *Between Give and Take: A Clinical Guide to Contextual Therapy* (New York: Brunner/Mazel, 1986); I. Boszormenyi-Nagi and G. Spark, *Invisible Partners* (New York: Brunner/Mazel, 1984); and I. Boszormenyi-Nagi and D. N. Ulrich, "Contextual Family Therapy," in *Handbook of Family Therapy,* ed. A. S. Gurman and D. P. Kniskern (New York: Brunner/Mazel, 1981), 159–86.

2. See Terry Hargrave and William Andersen, *Finishing Well: Aging and Reparation in the Intergenerational Family* (New York: Brunner/Mazel, 1992), 145–65.

3. See the Information Publication of the International Forgiveness Institute, Inc., P.O. Box 6153, Madison, WI 53716-0153, and the web page at http://www.forgiveness-institute.org/info &_ed.html. See also Gary Thomas, "The Forgiveness Factor," *Christianity Today* 44, no. 1 (January 10, 2000): 38–45.

4. Robert D. Enright, Elizabeth A. Gassin, and Ching-Ru Wu, "Forgiveness: A Developmental View," *Journal of Moral Education* 21, no. 2 (1992): 100.

5. Quotes in this section are from the Forgiveness Institute's website: www.forgiveness-institute.org/process_model_of_forgiveness_html.

6. For a full treatment of this issue, see Robert D. Enright and The Human Development Study Group, "The Moral Development of Forgiveness," in *Moral Behavior and Development,* ed. W. Kurtiness and J. Gewirtz (Hillsdale, N.J.: Erlbaum, 1991), 1:23–52. See also Enright, Gassin, and Wu, "Forgiveness," 99–114.

CHAPTER 3

A Theology of Being Human

∾

ARISING FROM THE FAITH of ancient Israel, the Christian tradition is founded on the long sweep of humanity's struggle with God's covenant and the reality of a God who became human to reveal the possibilities of becoming new creations. If the covenant made by Yahweh with Yahweh's people had not been broken through human choice, believers would have no need of the inspiration of the Christian scriptures. These holy books record and celebrate the journey in faith that acknowledges the sinful and broken dimension of human lives and, at the same time, provide direction to restore and heal covenantal love that has been torn asunder. To respond to the complexities of the stories of fractured relationships described earlier, this chapter will first consider the importance and implications of God's choice to make woman and man in God's own image as free human beings. Next, this chapter will view the importance and implications of sin and grace as intertwining realities that motivate and require repentance from hurtful, self-depreciating, and interpersonally wounding patterns of behavior. Finally, this chapter will investigate the importance and implications of God-made-human as a guide to a deepening understanding of a theology of being human together.

IMAGO DEI: MADE IN GOD'S IMAGE

The very essence of the Christian teaching about being human is the conviction that God desires and fashions each human being in God's own image. Every person is a reflection of the *imago dei;* each human

being bears the very imprint of God's own life. In the initial event nar-
rated in Genesis, God says, "Let us make humanity in our own image,
after our likeness. . . . God created humanity in the image of God, male
and female God created them. . . . God looked at everything God had
made, and found it very good" (Gen. 1:26–27, 31). Before humanity's
fall and original sin, there was and is "original blessing." Man and
woman, male and female, were and are created to project the divine
image, and their very being is uniquely wedded in intimacy to their
Creator. The first two chapters of Genesis teach believers that human
existence is a gift from a Creator and creative God. Jane Kopas says,
"Membership in the human species determines all human beings as
bearers of the image of God, no human being lacks it."[1] The gift of life
comes with the charge to steward, tend, and share in the responsibility for the created world. The blessing of life and the call to partner-
ship with God in the creative care of the earth come with the
additional blessing of the company of others with whom to share the
community of interpersonal and social companionship. Father John
Sachs, S.J., says, "Human persons are spiritual, embodied creatures
who, above all, are blessed with freedom which, guided by conscience
comes to fulfillment in love of God and neighbor."[2]

> "Let us make humanity in our own image, after our like-
> ness. . . . God created humanity in the image of God, male
> and female God created them. . . . God looked at every-
> thing God had made, and found it very good." (Gen.
> 1:26–27, 31)

Both creation accounts in Genesis 1–2 underscore the biblical truth
that the dignity of each person is rooted and routed in *community* with
others. The biblical truism that "it is not good for man [woman] to be
alone" (Gen. 2:18) is indeed the basis for the thesis of developmental
psychology that human persons grow into the fullness of their humanity within the web of caring human relationships. It is also a psychological tenet that all humans will face psychosocial developmental
crises in their striving toward maturity.[3] Developmental psychology,
similar to Christian conviction, holds the notion that "crises create
character." Healthy character formation with attention to sexual differentiation is a wonderful example of the essential relationality and
interdependence human beings share. Father Sachs explains:

Therefore, no human being can claim to experience or understand the mystery of what it means to be human only from his or her humanity. The real humanity of each person, male or female, is something that points beyond itself to a real other. This is a paradox. Male and female are not simply accidental characteristics of human being; neither are they two different creatures. They are irreducibly different in one humanity.[4]

Gender differentiation emphasizes the essentially relational character of each human being.

One theological definition of what it means to be human suggests that the human person is the receptive, spiritually alive being created with an innate desire to strive toward growth in the direction of the Creator, who is the horizon of human becoming and human destiny. In Christian thinking, the human being is the place of God's free message of unconditional love, and eminent Catholic theologian Karl Rahner, S.J., notes that the human person is "the being who possesses the infinity of absolute spiritual openness for becoming . . . who alone possesses the capacity for the eternal."[5] There is a dynamism within the natural fabric of the human experience that presses the human being in the direction of the Divine as humans strive for wholeness and fulfillment through their capacity for relational self-transcending love. God's own creative freedom is not exhausted by the creation of finite and fragile beings who, in spite of their possessing the capacity to know and love God, cannot fully comprehend the wisdom, insight, hope, depth, and scope of the fullness of God's nature and activity (Eph. 1:17-20).

> *The human person is "the being who possesses the infinity of absolute spiritual openness for becoming . . . who alone possesses the capacity for the eternal."*

Human beings as wondrous projectors of God's own image in finitude and frailty are a mystery at the heart of a theology of being human together. Central to the biblical understanding of God's desire in creation is the fashioning of man and woman in God's image as original blessings and co-partners with God in the mystery of creation. The reality of the consequences of the broken covenant and its resultant oppressions, alienations, separations, and origins of sin must be seen in the context of the absolute gift of human freedom.

FREEDOM

Freedom is an essential and irrevocable constituent element of human nature. Self-determination and self-actualization are fundamental to human nature. Human beings possess the power and responsibility to share the direction and destiny of their own lives. Sadly, this gift of freedom also provides the condition for the possibility of exercising the capacity to hurt and abuse others. It is indeed within the context of human freedom that a perpetrator has the ability to choose evil with the consequent result of harming others. Human beings make mistakes and miss the mark with one another because of their inherent capacity to decide and act with freedom of choice. The exercise of human freedom creates the situation in which forgiveness becomes necessary.

Human freedom allows the offended to choose a response when faced with the situation of betrayal, broken trust, or any fracture in a relationship. Because of the element of human freedom, people have options in facing and overcoming the painful situations that require forgiveness, repentance, and reconciliation. Some victims may choose to hold a grudge to justify their pain and to remain in the victim status. Others may choose to face into the hurt and follow a path toward facing the wrongdoer directly with the hope of forgiveness and reconciliation. Human freedom permits the offender to choose to listen to the offended and hear about the consequences the offender's actions had on the one injured. Human freedom allows the offender to uncover and discover her or his responsibility in the hurt and to seek ways to restore the relationship. Repentance is an option within the repertoire of human actions. Certainly human beings are free to engage in a process together to determine how to proceed with a fractured relationship and to choose how the relationship can be lived in the future. Theologically speaking, humans manifest the gift of freedom through the experience of decisions made every day.

Human beings are moral agents with the innate potency to exert and express ourselves through the exercise of free choice. Every human being possesses a drive toward self-realization. This means that each of us is primarily responsible in adulthood for our own growth in becoming and developing our unique potential as a being-in-relationship. We live this primary responsibility within the sphere of our interpersonal relationships and a social milieu of shared obligations and entitlements. A theology of freedom is supported by contemporary psychological insights that suggest that we possess the potentiality of realizing ourselves in and through our experience of relationship.

Obviously, severe self-debilitating environmental situations such as child abuse or other forms of physical and psychic neglect often result in a distorted moral agency and the possible inability on the part of such persons to achieve their potential. These persons do not bear primary responsibility for their failure to thrive and grow into adult maturity. Sadly, these individuals are victims of the cycle of abuse far too familiar in contemporary American culture. Nevertheless, even those human beings quite debilitated from trauma and abuse can meaningfully participate in interpersonal life and at least can share limited responsibility for dealing with the brokenness that marks and mars their lives, even though such individuals do not bear the same moral culpability and capability as others raised in healthier, more nurturing environments. Untreated psychological disorders, as well, can and do cause considerable human hurt. Such circumstances, for example, may indeed exonerate someone from the imperatives of the gospel mandate of the forgiveness exchange. Even for such persons, however, the forgiveness exchange provides a path to resolving their hurt and breaking the cycle of abuse.

The pursuit of healthy, growth-filled, mutual relations is never easy because of the complexity and plight of the human situations that enmesh all humans. The insights and challenges being explored in this chapter accept the flawed human condition that all persons experience in their lifetimes. Threats to growth and self-actualization and inevitable yet unexpected painful situations are part of the human drama called life. The majority of people, including Marilyn, Bill, Marge, Susan, Jack, Steven, and Joseph, are not exempt from the consequences of their choices and decisions, life-giving or flawed as they may be. In view of the complexity of human relationships, how do the realities of sin and grace illumine the path into and through the experience of fractured covenants of love and trust?

THE MYSTERY AND REALITY OF SIN

A culture that overvalues and excessively encourages individuality, avoidance, and flight from interpersonal and social responsibility can produce citizens anesthetized to their own culpability and predisposed to see neither their own personal deterioration nor the impact of their choices on others. In the Catholic Church before the renewal of the Second Vatican Council (1962–1965), for example, sin was viewed personalistically and legalistically. Sin was a personal infraction of an external and objective law that resulted in a separation from God and neighbor. A focus on personal guilt and degrees of culpability for specific actions was often taken to the extreme of scrupulosity, while motives and intentions eluded the penitent.[6] The pre-Vatican II understanding of the sacrament of Penance, commonly called Confession, obliged a repentant sinner to make a sincere confession of all sinful infractions, venial and mortal, and receive a penance, most often a contrite recitation of prayers that followed receiving the blessing of absolution from the priest. The grace of the sacrament was dispensed with the absolution by the priest in the anonymous confines of a confessional. Commenting on the still emerging post-Vatican II understanding of the sacrament, theologian Sister Carol Frances Jegen, B.V.M., says, "A legalistic mentality which viewed sin as a matter of transgressing laws was being replaced by an understanding of sin as that which hurts persons, especially the one who sins."[7]

Without losing the stress on individual "acts" of sinfulness, the renewal of the sacrament of Penance, now known as the sacrament of Reconciliation, emphasizes the need for healing and reconciliation in the interpersonal and social dimensions of human behaviors. The theology of the sacrament of Reconciliation stresses that believers consider the motives and patterns of behavior that result in the ruptures of trust and love in interpersonal relations. This renewed sacramental understanding encourages persons to deeply examine their ways of relating, their attitudes, and their actions, intended or unintended, whose consequences produce suffering. Persons' "unconsciousness" regarding their free choices does not shelter them from responsibility for the consequences of their free choices. Critical examination also requires the individual to explore personal complicity in the larger structures and systems of society that demean or oppress or exploit either people or creation itself. The Christian understanding of sin now extends beyond the accumulation of personal guilt to the interpersonal, social, and systematic realization of human accommodation to and complicity with any form of inhumanity or crimes against the earth, such as racism or ecological destruction.

> *"A legalistic mentality which viewed sin as a matter of transgressing laws was being replaced by an understanding of sin as that which hurts persons, especially the one who sins."*

The theology and practice of the Roman Catholic sacrament of Reconciliation pose a challenge to a critically conscious manner of living. Sin is basically understood as the inevitable human frailty of not being continuously perfect. Sin is seen as consciously or unconsciously falling into patterns that "miss the mark" and cause the runner in faith to stumble. Sin is living in estrangement from one's essence, seriously disorients right relations, and has interpersonal and social consequences. Living in relationally sinful patterns necessarily results in a falling away from right, just, and reciprocal relationships. Hardness of heart ensues with ungraced resistance to critical self-examination. Sin pushes a person egocentrically inward, spiritually backward, and ultimately deathward (the real meaning of the term *mortal sin*).

These considerations confront believers with their responsibility to examine their own complicity in sinful patterns in interpersonal life, social relations, and social consciousness. In the era when sin was understood as individually act-based and an infraction of a moral law that was erased through intrapsychic contrition and sacramental Penance, confessional lines were long and Catholic persons were required to be in the necessary state of grace to receive Communion. During the last thirty-five years since the renewal of the sacrament, few seem drawn to the benefits of the sacrament of Reconciliation. This lack of interest may be due to a resistance to embracing the interpersonal and social examination that is now an essential part of the preparation for engaging in the sacrament of Reconciliation. The change in name from Penance to Reconciliation represents a shift in emphasis often misunderstood by laity and clergy alike. Reconciliation differs from Confession in the same way that interpersonal processes differ from intrapsychic processes. Reconciliation is experienced in the context of relationship. The renewed sacrament of Reconciliation offers the penitent the option of engaging in face-to-face dialogue with the priest. Seminary preparation to become an adept and compassionate minister of the sacrament may not always provide priests with the depth and scope of interpersonal skill necessary to administer an interpersonal sacrament. Lack of understanding and training also leads to confusion and conflict around the experience and necessity of the sacrament in living the Christian life to the full.

The emphasis on the multidimensional nature of forgiveness is congruent with the theological conviction that sin is an inevitable part of human freedom in being human together, just as the reality of grace is God's continuous gift aimed at the restoration of love torn asunder. The Christian message is the "good news" that the world in its fallenness and frailty—rife with egoism, injustice, and mass suffering—is not the world God intended in God's wondrous activity of creation. The covenant, though broken by human failure, endures because God is faithful from generation to generation.

GRACE

In any discussion of human frailty and failure, grace is essential. Grace is the present and future gift of God's favor, the universal and timeless offer of God's love into eternity, the power to change, and a participation in divine life here and now. Grace assists the person's striving to grow through all the seasons of life. Grace is the ever-available gift of Godlife that holds the spiritual key to support humans in transcending the flawed tendencies toward self-absorption, estrangement from personal essence, and hardness of heart. A long-standing conviction is that grace builds on nature. The relevance of this conviction in faith is that the person in all his or her frailty can, if he or she remains open, change patterns of hurtful living to new ways of offering and receiving healing. The reality of grace means that God never ceases to give Godself in intimacy to those whom God has breathed into being. Openness to receiving the power and tenderness of grace can result in the willingness to release silently held grudges by entering into honest conversation or allow entrenched egoism to be gradually replaced by

> *Grace is the present and future gift of God's favor, the universal and timeless offer of God's love into eternity, the power to change, and a participation in divine life here and now.*

a new mutuality. Offended and offender alike become freed and restored persons by the action of grace that moves each to embrace the gift and task of the forgiveness exchange.

The ever-abundant presence of the ongoing gift of God's life, grace, is available in and through the actual experiences of daily living. The time of grace is always at hand. All humans created in God's image participate in God's life here and now to the degree that each freely and consciously chooses to engage the relationship. Humans possess the divine spark and are already blessed as God's daughters and sons here and now. The divine spark residing and hiding within each person holds the mystery of individual human destiny that already exists within the essence of each person. Grace is God's free and enduring gift to enable human becoming in the image of God. This means that the task of self-realization in and through the gift of human relationships cannot be avoided. In spite of all the obstacles and betrayals life presents, human beings in freedom and grace are either moving in the direction of becoming in God or in the direction of a self-refusal toward the endlessly gifting God. From a theological perspective, our daily living is never neutral.

> *"The mainstream Catholic tradition has always been insistent that the grace of God is given to us, not to make up for something lacking to us human persons, but as a free gift that elevates us to a new and unmerited level of existence."*

The choice to face the many opportunities to give and receive forgiveness is ever before believers. Because humans are created free and are the recipients of God's persistent offer of grace, each person bears the responsibility to shape her or his moral destiny, a destiny necessarily intertwined with others. The painful realities of life do not always reflect the life God intended for humans in creation. Catholic theologian Richard McBrien states, "The mainstream Catholic tradition has always been insistent that the grace of God is given to us, not to make up for something lacking to us humans persons, but as a free gift that elevates us to a new and unmerited level of existence."[8] Grace, then, is the gift that helps humans respond to the reality of living God's life abundantly even amidst human frailty and flaws. Christians embrace the belief that in and through Jesus, God entered and redeemed the human experience.

JESUS: GOD'S DESIRE FOR IMMERSION IN HUMANITY

That God became flesh in Jesus of Nazareth is a central Christian theological conviction. God became human. In Jesus, God's free decision to enter the human experience is revealed once in time for all time. Theologian Karl Rahner reminds Christians that in Jesus, God spoke the final, definitive, all-inclusive, and absolutely irrevocable Word. God uttered this word into the world so that God cannot recall it. God has spoken God's own eternal Word in the very flesh of humanity. God has created an "irrevocable face" through the Word's remaining the Word of God yet becoming a real part of the world. McBrien says, "Because of the incarnation, God is in humankind and remains so for all eternity, and humankind is for all eternity the expression of the mystery of God because the whole human race has been assumed in the individual human reality of Jesus."[9] The mystery of the Incarnation is that God can give Godself away and yet not become less in the giving. Jesus reveals the nature of God's love. The God of history extolled in the pages of the Hebrew Scriptures is born human through the yes of the woman Mary. Jesus is the symbol, sacrament, and servant of human redemption.

Jesus Christ is symbol in that he is the ultimate self-utterance of God; the one who points the way to the encounter with the wholly Other: *Abba*.[10] Jesus is sacrament because he effects what he symbolizes. He brings about the redemption he reveals, and the reign of God is intimated through his very life, death, and resurrection. Jesus is servant in that he witnesses to God's free choice in love to enter the world as human. Jesus embraces the toll of suffering and calls others to see it as more than what it appears to be.

> *God stands with the offended in the midst of her or his suffering.*

God chose to self-disclose in the world where humans are most at home. God gave Godself to humanity in direct proximity. For the

Christian, all ways of meeting this God are personal. The decision to take on the flesh and blood of the human experience makes divinity tangible and reconsecrates humanity in the glory of *imago dei*. For the Christian, the ongoing gift of God's life as grace is made irrevocably tangible in Jesus. Christians see in Jesus the actualization of the life of grace amidst tremendous challenges. The gospel of Jesus is testimony to the power and promise of grace alive in human freedom and moving people from so many forms of bondage to liberation, from sickness in body and spirit to healing, from alienation to community, from darkness to light, and from despair to hope.

Because Jesus is both the historical and timeless embodiment of God's desire for immersion in humanity, the Christian possesses the ultimate reminder of the absolute and irrevocable interpersonal nature of God. Jesus of Nazareth, the mystery of the Incarnation, brought the transcendence of God into the immanence of human experience. God's covenant with humanity is essentially interpersonal. Christian theology refers to the Incarnation as the relational intersection of the transcendent with the imminent. God made flesh. The implication of the mystery and the doctrine of the Incarnation are invaluable to a discussion of interpersonal forgiveness.

God stands with the offended in the midst of her or his suffering. The one injured is not alone in the pain and confusion. *Abba* understands the cost of the undeserved embrace of the cross. God's grace is present to strengthen, encourage, and direct a healing action. At the same time, the offender does not stand alone amidst the accusation and the ruptured relationship. God stands with the offender to affirm the worth of the wrongdoer as *imago dei* even as she or he is called in accountability to face the consequences of the intended or unintended offense. In an unsuccessful forgiveness exchange, the offended can transfer the responsibility of forgiveness to God, who is an intimate partner in the relationship. God can hold the offender accountable. This notion of the incarnate Jesus—God made human—as the third party of the forgiveness exchange is revealed in Matthew 18:20, where Jesus is recorded as saying, "Where two or three are gathered in my name, there am I in the midst of them." The good news of the Christian message is that no one is ever bereft of the God who promises to be with us forever. In the closing chapters of the Gospel of John, Jesus makes ready for his departure and promises a Counselor to come, the Spirit of truth, who will dwell within those who believe (John 14:12–

18). Such is the nature of the imminent dimension of an incarnate God at work in the midst of the blessings and challenges of the redeeming activity of forgiveness, repentance, and reconciliation.

APPLICATION

Christians seek to follow the Way and ways of Jesus, who says, "Enter through the narrow gate. The gate that leads to damnation is wide, the road is clear, and many choose to travel it. But how narrow is the gate that leads to life, how rough the road, and how few there are who find it!" (Matt. 7:13–14). The narrow gate is, of course, a metaphor for the humanly challenging, grace-filled path toward God's kingdom. The kingdom of God is realized here and now, albeit partially, in and through the Christian practice of repentance, forgiveness, and reconciliation. These realities are part and parcel of the gift of being human together.

A biblically based and theologically sound vision of the human person is a fundamentally optimistic way of looking at human nature and human potentials. Human beings possess the capacity to develop, even if on a restricted basis, the abilities for critical self-examination and the power to transcend their limits. Reflectively read the following verses from the first book of the Bible, Genesis 1:26–27, 31, and consider the following questions.

+ How does my life give positive witness to the truth in faith that every human being is an image of God?

+ Am I aware of attitudes and actions that demean others because I view them as inherently less worthy?

+ Our desire and capacity for intellectual, physical, emotional, and spiritual growth are seeded within us. We are innately drawn in the direction of becoming free and loving individuals. Life presents unforeseen obstacles, often not of our own making, that block our sense of personal, interpersonal, professional, and social well-being. Yet the gift of human freedom holds the potential for facing into and overcoming much of what inhibits our growth.

+ In what ways and under what circumstances have I experienced the exercise of human freedom that resulted in breaking through an impasse? Do I experience myself as more prone to feeling victimized by the difficulties that surface in my life and to wishing that others could and should make my life better? Do I experience myself as more disposed toward taking an active role in dealing directly with obstacles that impede my sense of freedom and well-being?

♦ Have I developed sufficient self-critical honesty to explore my motives and patterns of behavior to access my complicity in the impasses and obstacles that arise in my life?

♦ Is my usual *modus operandi* to place blame outside myself and project my dissatisfaction for my plight upon others? When this trajectory emerges, what processes do I employ to make sure that my judgments are fair, accurate, constructive, and productive?

Sin is understood as the inevitable human frailty of not being continuously perfect.

Sin is falling into patterns of attitude and behavior that "miss the mark" and result in some form of fracture in relationship.

Sin is living in estrangement from one's essence, disorients right relations, and always has interpersonal and social consequences.

Sin is revealed in patterns of attitude and action whose consequences disrupt reciprocity in relationship, produce hardness of heart, and resist critical self-examination.

Unattended Sin will continue to push a person egocentrically inward, spiritually backward, and ultimately deathward (the real meaning of the term *mortal sin*).

♦ Which of the above phrases captures a felt understanding of the reality of sin in your life?

♦ Enter in your journal a free-flowing and uncensored description of how sin operates in your life.

> *Grace* is God's free and enduring gift to enable human becoming in the image of God.
>
> *Grace* enables humans to transcend their flawed tendencies toward self-absorption.
>
> *Grace* helps humans respond to the reality of living God's life abundantly even amidst human frailty and flaws.

♦ Reflect on those occasions when you have been most aware of God's grace.

♦ What areas of your life are in need of God's grace?

♦ Enter in your journal a free-flowing and uncensored description of how God's grace operates in your life.

NOTES

1. Jane Kopas, *Sacred Identity: Exploring a Theology of the Person* (New York: Paulist Press, 1994), 143.

2. John Sachs, *The Christian Vision of Humanity: Basic Christian Anthropology* (Collegeville, Minn.: Liturgical Press, 1991), 9.

3. Erik Erikson charted eight stages of psychosocial development: (1) trust versus mistrust, (2) autonomy versus shame or doubt, (3) initiative versus guilt, (4) industry versus inferiority, (5) identity versus identity/role diffusion/confusion, (6) intimacy versus self-absorption/isolation, (7) generativity versus stagnation, and (8) integrity versus despair. For a detailed description of these stages, see Erik Erikson, *Childhood and Society* (New York: W. W. Norton, 1950), 219–34; and *Identity and the Life Cycle* (New York: W. W. Norton, 1980), 54–82.

4. Sachs, *Christian Vision*, 20.

5. Gerald A. McCool, ed., *A Rahner Reader* (New York: Seabury Press, 1975), 24.

6. Monica Hellwig, *What Are the Theologians Saying Now?* (Westminster, Md.: Christian Classics, 1992), 107.

7. Carol Frances Jegen, *Restoring Our Friendship with God: The Mystery of Redemption from Suffering and Sin* (Wilmington, Del.: Michael Glazier, 1989), 39.

8. Richard McBrien, *Catholicism* (San Francisco: Harper Collins, 1994), 169.

9. Ibid., 498.

10. *Abba* is the Aramaic word recorded in the Gospels as one of the words Jesus used to speak of Yahweh. This word expressed the very intimate relationship Jesus experienced with God and was used to address God in early Christian communities. See Galatians 4:6 and Romans 8:15.

CHAPTER 4

Biblical Confrontation and Accountability

∿

ONFRONTATION IS SO FRIGHTENING that the vast majority of us humans avoid it at all costs. Indeed, facing our offenders and challenging their harmful or hurtful conduct makes us vulnerable once again to the actions of our offender. Fear of shame, ridicule, or rejection often paralyzes us into a strained silence that only transparently masks the damaged or broken relationship between us and our offender. Our human aversion to admitting and owning faults, shortcomings, or failures in relationships confirms our fear of confrontation, and human history is littered with the wounded and dead who dared to confront. Confronting is risky business, and many of us understandably quote the Bible to legitimate our avoidance of confrontation.

BIBLICAL EXCUSES TO AVOID CONFRONTATION

Frequently, those of us who avoid confrontation appeal to Jesus' prohibition "Judge not lest you be judged" in Matt. 7:1//Luke 6:37 as an excuse to avoid confrontation.[1] Since confronting requires judging or determining the conduct of another to be unjust, we conclude that Jesus' absolute prohibition against judging also excludes confrontation. Indeed, a surface reading of Jesus' prohibition apart from its literary form and context apparently supports this conclusion. Nevertheless, both the form and the context of this prohibition argue against this use of Jesus' prohibition as a sanction for avoiding confrontation.

> *"Judge not lest you be judged." (Matt. 7:1)*
>
> *Cast in the form of a general maxim that is impossible to apply absolutely and comprehensively, Jesus' prohibition impels us to consider the appropriate application.*

Jesus' prohibition is in the form of a general maxim whose specific application requires prudence and discernment. Those who oppose confrontation want to apply the maxim to every specific case as a prohibition against all types of judging. Applying the maxim in this way, however, establishes an impractical and unattainable ideal. No human relationship or society has ever existed in which some standards of conduct were not expected and enforced. Such a relationship or society is even inconceivable because of flawed human nature. Eventually in every relationship, a person is disappointed with the behavior of another. Refusing to judge this behavior as inadequate by ignoring it and sanctioning it with silence leads not to resolution but to an increased strain on the relationship. Humans do assess words and deeds every day as an essential activity of being human, and Jesus himself did not reserve judgment on several occasions. Thus, applying this maxim to every specific case, as some of us wish to do, is impossible because of human nature and the dynamics of relationship.

Cast in the form of a general maxim that is impossible to apply absolutely and comprehensively, Jesus' prohibition impels us to consider the appropriate application. This maxim is not an exemption from thinking so that the maxim is applied indiscriminately to every case but rather a vivid invitation for us to determine when and how judgment both is and is not proper. H. D. Betz astutely recognizes the force of this maxim by saying, "The question is not whether one should abandon judging altogether; rather, the point is that good judgment is a necessary element in human relations."[2] The context that follows Jesus' prohibition in Matthew's Gospel explains when and how good judgment is attained and bad judgment avoided.

Few who quote Jesus' prohibition against judging in Matthew 7:1 include the remainder of the passage. The very next verse (Matt. 7:2) states the reason for the prohibition as "for by the standard you are judging, you shall be judged, and by the measure you are measuring, it shall be measured to you."[3] This reason shifts the focus from not judging at all to judging with standardized norms that apply both to the one judging and to the one being judged. Indeed, justice requires that the norms or standards be applied equally and impartially to all. Thus, the explanation in this verse indicates that Jesus' prohibition against judging is not an absolute prohibition but a call for just and equitable judgment.

> *"Why do you notice the splinter in your brother's (or sister's) eye, but do not perceive the wooden beam in your own eye?" (Matt. 7:3)*

The rhetorical question in the next verse (Matt. 7:3) confirms this understanding of Jesus' prohibition. Jesus asks, "Why do you notice the splinter in your brother's (or sister's) eye, but do not perceive the wooden beam in your own eye?" The exaggeration in this question emphasizes that the prohibition against judging is actually a prohibition against judging unfairly with a duplicitous standard. We should not hold another to a more rigorous standard than we ourselves are willing to accept. Jesus calls the person judging with such duplicity a hypocrite and recommends such a person first apply the standard of judgment to his or her own life (Matt. 7:5). Then Jesus says, "You will see clearly to remove the splinter from your brother's (or sister's) eye." Instead of prohibiting judgment, Jesus recommends perceiving and removing the faults of others, but only after we submit ourselves to the same standards of judgment. Rather than prohibiting confrontation as the opponents of confrontation suggest, Jesus' prohibition against judging in Matt. 7:1 and his subsequent explanation actually recommend confrontation provided those of us who confront submit to the same standard of conduct that we expect from others.

In addition to Jesus' prohibition against judging, those of us who resist confrontation sometimes appeal to Jesus' charge of hypocrisy in Matt. 7:5 and elsewhere as a sanction for avoiding confrontation. Since no one is perfect, some of us often charge others of us courageous enough to confront as being hypocrites. This charge attempts to disarm us as confronters and to derail the confrontation process by shifting the focus from the deeds of the offender to our own deeds as confronters so as to shame us into silence. This strategy, however, does not lead to resolution of conflicts and to healthy relationships or societies, and neither Jesus nor any biblical text uses the charge of hypocrisy as a sanction for avoiding confrontation.

The modern understanding of *hypocrite* as someone who is not perfect but nevertheless dares to mention the fault of another is even absent from the Hebrew and Christian scriptures. These texts never designate someone who confronts as a hypocrite. Instead, the word *hypocrite* denotes the godless, the transgressor, or the lawless.[4] From its use in Greek culture to designate a theatrical actor or actress, some Jewish and Christian texts use the word with the meaning *pretender*, someone whose outward actions or speech are inconsistent with her or his inward intentions, thoughts, and essence (2 Macc. 5:25; 6:21–25; 4 Macc. 6:15–23; Luke 20:20). Often the metaphor of the discrepancy between lips and heart expresses this meaning of *hypocrite* (Isa. 29:13; Sir. 1:25–29; Mark 7:6; Matt. 15:7). These texts condemn as hypocrites those who worship God with ulterior motives (Matt. 6:2, 5, 16; *Pss. Sol.* 4:6, 22) and especially those frauds or impostors who falsely interpret God's laws and ways (Matt. 23:13–36; *Pss. Sol.* 4:6, 8). The absence of the modern understanding of hypocrite in these texts removes the charge of hypocrisy as a biblical sanction for avoiding confrontation, and those of us who resist confrontation should refrain from using this charge to derail the confrontation process by disarming others of us who need to confront.

Alongside Jesus' prohibition against judging and his charge of hypocrisy, many who resist confrontation also use Jesus' recommendation of turning the other cheek in Matt. 5:39 as a sanction for not confronting. Again, Jesus' statement is rarely quoted in context. The entire passage (Matt. 5:38–42) reads:

> You have heard that it was said, "An eye for an eye and a tooth for a tooth." But I tell you not to retaliate against the evildoer. Instead: whoever strikes you on your right cheek, turn to him (or her) the other also; and to the one who wants to go to court with you and take your undergarment, let him (or her) have also your outer garment. And whoever will press you into service for one mile, go with (that person) two. To the one who asks you, give; and from the one who wants to borrow from you, do not turn away.[5]

The literary and historical contexts of this passage argue against using it as a sanction for avoiding confrontation.

Jesus is instructing his disciples about the appropriate application of the *lex talionis*, the law of retaliation, in their specific situation of

Roman domination. In 4 B.C.E., the Romans detached Galilee from Judea, levied tribute, and established client rulers over each region. In 6 C.E., the Romans annexed Judea to the Roman Province of Syria and began taxing it directly. Judas, a Galilean, led a revolt that was ruthlessly crushed by the Romans, who crucified Judas along with two thousand of his followers. Various Jewish resistance groups appeared until both Galilee and Judea revolted against the Romans in 66 C.E.

> *"Whoever strikes you on your right cheek, turn to him (or her) the other also. . . . Whoever will press you into service for one mile, go with (that person) two." (Matt. 5:38–42)*

In this historical situation, applying the law of retaliation is impractical and disastrous. Instead, Jesus advises his followers not to resist the Romans but to turn the other cheek when slapped, since slapping those in authority even in retaliation is most unwise. Jesus advises his followers to be generous toward the dominant by being willing to give the outer garment to the one who sues for the undergarment and by going an extra mile when impressed to go one mile. Being commandeered to go one mile refers to a Roman institution that permitted Roman soldiers to impress civilians to serve as couriers. The Roman soldiers in charge of Jesus' crucifixion applied this institution to Simon of Cyrene, who was forced to carry Jesus' cross (Mark 15:21//Matt. 27:32). Jesus advises giving to the one who asks and lending to the one who requests a loan. Resistance groups were reticent to do either of these for Romans or for Roman sympathizers. By refusing to retaliate and by being generous, Jesus advises his group to foster relations with dominant persons that expediently avoid the dangers of antagonism and resistance.

Seen in its literary and historical contexts, Jesus' recommendation of turning the other cheek in Matt. 5:39 does not provide us with a sanction for avoiding confrontation and passively suffering under the offenses of others. This recommendation occurs in a specific historical situation in which nonresistance was prudent. Certainly, Jesus' recommendation of nonresistance still applies to hostages, those under martial law, and others in positions of near powerlessness.[6] The universalization of this recommendation, however, is not prudent. Betz correctly states, "Ethically, there can be no question that total nonresistance to evil constitutes an irrational and unjustifiable position incompatible with the rest of early Christian teaching and its numerous admonitions to combat, avoid, or escape from evil."[7]

CONFRONTATION AS THE APPROPRIATE RESPONSE

Neither Jesus' prohibition against judging nor his charge of hypocrisy nor his recommendation of nonresistance sanctions avoidance of confrontation. Instead, Jesus explicitly prescribes confrontation as the appropriate response toward offenders. According to Matt. 18:15–17, Jesus states, "If your brother (or sister) sins [against you], go and tell the fault between you and him (or her) alone" (Matt. 18:15a). Instead of recommending denial of the offense or forgiveness of the offender or sharing the offense with sympathizers as the initial response, Jesus recommends confrontation. When anyone perceives being wronged by another, the appropriate response is going to the other and explaining the perceived offense. Jesus' prescription of confrontation as the appropriate response toward our offenders could not be stated more clearly.

> *"If your brother (or sister) sins [against you], go and tell the fault between you and him (or her) alone." (Matt. 18:15)*

Jesus' prescription of confrontation as the appropriate response avoids the detrimental effects of other possible responses. Who among us has not tried to deny or ignore an offense or an offender at one time or another? When we do, we usually find that our efforts to sustain our denial disconnect us from the offense and generate inner turmoil that often results in depression. We expend large amounts of mental and emotional energy repressing the memory of the offense, but our denial is an unhealthy response that helps neither us nor the offender, who may continue to harm not only us but others in the community. Our denial is detrimental to both ourselves and those who offend us.

An increasing number of people are investing in the intrapsychic forgiveness process as an appropriate response to being deeply

wounded. Indeed, many books on forgiveness as well as counselors
and public speakers recommend that we forgo any efforts at confrontation and release our offenders from all accountability and especially from the obligation to repent. We are encouraged to modify our
thinking and release our negative feelings toward our offenders. When
we try forgiving in this way, we may discover that just when we think
we have forgiven, our offender reappears along with the painful feelings of the original wound. This type of intrapsychic forgiveness
demands from us significant energy to hold feelings of forgiveness in
place but demands from our offenders no effort to modify or even
recognize detrimental behavioral patterns. Relationships with our
offenders are one-sidedly maintained by this type of forgiveness, and
such relationships are not truly mutual. Restricting our response to
intrapsychic forgiveness alone may be detrimental to the well-being of
our relationships.

The majority of people, however, often take the path of least resistance and simply tell a sympathetic friend about being hurt. Our
motive is usually not to enlist our friend's help in devising a strategy
of confrontation and resolution of the conflict but simply to receive
sympathy so that we feel better and avoid the ominous threat of confronting the one who hurt us. An empathetic friend, in contrast, feels
worse and wonders what to do about the offender. Our more passive
friends will probably bear a silent grudge of ill feelings. Our more
active friends may verbally attack the offender on our behalf. Our
offender now feels offended and thinks our friends had no right to
such an attack. "After all," he or she reasons, "I did nothing to them."
In response to such an attack, our offender will of course seek allies,
and suddenly we find our social group at war. Quickly spreading the
problem to the entire community, our response dissolves the bonds of
trust and commitment between ourselves and our offenders and
divides the community between allegiance to us and them. Clearly,
our response is no way to treat either our friends or those who hurt
us.

Instead of these detrimental responses, Jesus prescribes confrontation. As frightening as confrontation may be, it is nevertheless the
most healthy and prudent response for us. Confrontation places the
initial responsibility on us as the offended to recognize and articulate
the offense. We must usually initiate the confrontation since our
offenders frequently either do not perceive the offense or do not feel

the same motivation to resolve the offense as we do. Feelings of being wronged usually persist and play over and over again in our mind. These feelings provide us with sufficient motivation to move toward resolution. Offenders usually lack such persistent feelings along with the motivation to resolve the situation. In cases when our offenders do recognize the offense and experience persistent remorse, they may still be reticent to approach us for fear of harming us once again. Confrontation appropriately places the initial responsibility on the one offended.

> *As frightening as confrontation may be, it is nevertheless the most healthy and prudent response for us.*

This responsibility encourages us to understand clearly and to state precisely the nature of the offense. Instead of generalizing or inflating the offense to unrealistic proportions, we place the offense in the context of our relationship with the offender. This contextualization provides boundaries for addressing and resolving the offense. Confrontation permits us to express our feelings and to "get it off our chest" but in a way that does not spread the problem to the broader community. Instead, we express the hurt specifically toward our offender who caused the hurt in the first place and who has the ability to respond in such a way that enables us to release the hurt.

Our expression of the hurt and the precise articulation of the offense now move the responsibility from us to our offender, who may either accept or reject the responsibility. Jesus says, "If the offender listens to you, you have won your brother (or sister). If the offender does not listen, take one or two others along with you, so that 'every fact may be established on the testimony of two or three witnesses'" (Matt. 18:15b–16). Our offender's rejection of responsibility elicits another round of confrontation. This time, however, the confrontation is not simply between us and our offender alone but a few other community members who are informed about the offense and accompany us in the confrontation process. If the offender remains obstinate in refusing to accept responsibility, the entire community now has the responsibility to confront. If the offender refuses to hear the community, Jesus recommends "treating him (or her) as you would a Gentile

> *"If the offender listens to you, you have won your brother (or sister). If the offender does not listen, take one or two others along with you, so that every fact may be established on the testimony of two or three witnesses." (Matt. 18:15b–16)*

or a tax collector" (Matt. 18:17b). Our offender is treated as one outside the community and as a candidate for conversion.

This series of confrontations brings increasing pressure to bear on the offender as more and more community members participate in the process. This increasing pressure of confrontation encourages the offender "to listen" and to own responsibility for her or his action. These confrontations strengthen the bonds of trust and commitment in the community as more and more members participate in the restoration of our offender and the resolution of the offense. If and when the matter must eventually become known to the entire community, an obstinate offender is so exposed that allegiance to her or him is difficult. Thus, the community is spared the divisive and detrimental effects of nonconfrontational responses. Even though it is frightening, confrontation provides the most healthy and prudent response to offenses, and not surprisingly Jesus explicitly prescribes confrontation as the appropriate response toward our offenders.

JESUS THE CONFRONTER

Jesus not only prescribes this response but he also practices it. Jesus does not simply forgive and ignore the offenses of his generation. Instead, he summons his generation to repent (Matt. 4:17) and predicts stern judgment upon the unrepentant (Matt. 10:14–15, 33, 37–39; 11:16–19, 20–24; 23:13–36). When his fellow citizens in Nazareth take offense at him, he does not suffer the affront silently but points out their failure by stating, "A prophet is not without honor except in his native place and in his own house" (Matt. 13:57). When some demand a sign to authenticate his message, Jesus responds, "An evil and unfaithful generation seeks a sign" (Matt. 12:38–39; 16:1–4). Recognizing that his generation is not responding appropriately to his confrontational preaching, Jesus states, "At the judgment, the men of Nineveh will arise with this generation and condemn it, because they repented at the preaching of Jonah; and there is something greater than Jonah here" (Matt. 12:41). Jesus confronts his generation and holds it accountable for its deeds.

> *Jesus not only prescribes confrontation; he also practices it.*

In addition to his general confrontational preaching, Jesus confronts specific groups in his generation such as the Pharisees with their scribes, the chief priests along with the elders, and the Sadducees. Jesus confronts Pharisees with their sins of omission. Jesus points out some Pharisees' lack of fruitfulness. In parabolic form, he recounts the story of tenants who refuse to give the landowner his produce (Matt. 21:33–41). These Pharisees correctly perceive that the parable applies to them (Matt. 21:45). Jesus points out that some Pharisees lack mercy and compassion and were quite willing to ignore the spiritual needs of those of questionable occupation and reputation (Matt. 9:11–13) as well as the physical needs of others (Matt. 12:1–14). When some Pharisees question Jesus about divorce, Jesus challenges their lack of mercy as demonstrated by their hardness of heart in divorcing their wives (Matt. 19:8). Jesus reminds these Pharisees of God's desire for the fruit of mercy and compassion (Matt. 9:13; 12:7; cf. Hos. 6:6).

In addition to their sins of omission, Jesus also confronts some Pharisees with their sins of commission. He challenges their evil orientation. After certain Pharisees accuse Jesus of casting out demons by Beelzebul, the prince of demons, Jesus responds that a tree is known by its fruit and characterizes these Pharisees as a "brood of vipers" who cannot say good things because they are evil (Matt. 12:34). He warns them that on the day of judgment, they will render an account for their words (Matt. 12:36–37). Certain other Pharisees plot to entrap Jesus by asking whether it is lawful to pay the census tax to Caesar (Matt. 22:15–22). Perceiving their malice, Jesus confronts them with their real intent to test him rather than to determine the lawfulness of the census tax (Matt. 22:18). Using "woes" common to prophetic and apocalyptic speech, Jesus confronts certain Pharisees with their scribes for their obstructionism (Matt. 23:13–14), misguided missionary zeal (Matt. 23:15), deluded casuistry (Matt. 23:16–22), and hypocritical piety (Matt. 23:23–36; cf. Matt. 15:1–9). Jesus considered these actions unacceptable and confronted Pharisees guilty of these sins of commission.

Jesus not only confronts Pharisees but also the chief priests along with the elders. As with the Pharisees, Jesus points out the fruitlessness of the chief priests in the parable of the Tenants (Matt. 21:33–46). He confronts them with their ignorance of the scriptures (Matt. 21:12–17) and exposes their political duplicity in refusing to express their opinion about the origin of John's baptism (Matt. 21:23–27). Jesus challenges their disbelief of John's message and warns that prostitutes and tax collectors are preceding them into the kingdom (Matt. 21:23–32). Perhaps the most serious fault Jesus confronts is the chief priests' persistent failure to repent and change their minds about believing John's message of righteousness (Matt. 21:32).

In contrast to Jesus' repeated confrontations with the Pharisees and chief priests, he only confronts Sadducees once according to the canonical Gospels. These Sadducees, who do not believe in a resurrection of the dead, recount the story of a woman successively married to seven brothers according to the law of the levirate.[8] These Sadducees then ask Jesus whose wife she would be in the resurrection. They expect Jesus to abandon belief in the resurrection of the dead because of the impossibility of determining her one legal husband since all were legal husbands. Jesus pointedly replies, "You are misled because you do not know the scriptures or the power of God" (Matt. 22:29). Jesus explains that the scriptures affirm a resurrection of the dead and that God has the power to effect such a resurrection. Thus, Jesus confronts these Sadducees with their error arising from their ignorance of scripture and God.

APPLICATION

These examples of Jesus' confrontation demonstrate that Jesus consistently follows his prescribed response to those who fall short in their relationships. Jesus not only prescribes confrontation but also practices it. Confrontation may indeed be frightening, but none of Jesus' sayings legitimates our avoidance of confrontation. Instead, Jesus both prescribes and practices confrontation as the appropriate response to our offenders.

- ◆ Reflect on the various "biblical" excuses for avoiding confrontation. Which excuse have you most often used—the prohibition against judging, the charge of hypocrisy, or the exhortation to turn the other cheek?

- ◆ Which of these excuses have been used against you to force you into a strained silence that only masks the damaged or broken relationship?

- ◆ When hurt or let down by another, what is your usual response? Do you tell a sympathetic friend about your hurt? Do you try to deny or ignore the offense? Do you try to forgive your offender intrapsychically? What has been the result of any of these strategies you have tried?

- ◆ When hurt or let down by another, have you tried Jesus' recommendation of confrontation? What was the result?

- ◆ Are you comfortable with a confrontational Jesus? Have you previously perceived Jesus in this way? Do you prefer a kinder, gentler Jesus?

- ◆ Are you a confronter? If so, how does Jesus' model of confrontation affect you? If not, does the model of Jesus as a confronter challenge you?

- ◆ Complete the following "unfinished sentence" with the first "unfiltered" response that comes to your mind.

    I think the best response to an offender is . . . .

NOTES

1. The discussion that follows relies primarily on the Matthean portrait of Jesus.

2. H. D. Betz, *The Sermon on the Mount: A Commentary on the Sermon on the Mount including the Sermon on the Plain (Matthew 5:3–7:27 and Luke 6:20–49,* Hermeneia (Minneapolis: Fortress, 1995), 487.

3. In the structure of this clause, the nominal form of "to judge" occurs as the object of a preposition that modifies the verb "to judge." In this construc-

tion, the nominal form expresses the standard or norm by which the judgment is rendered. A similar construction occurs in Num. 35:24, which the RSV translates, "The congregation shall judge . . . in accordance with these ordinances [norms or standards]."

4. For examples of "hypocrite" meaning "godless," see Job 15:34; Isa. 33:14; and Prov. 11:9 in Aquila's, Symmachus's, and Theodotion's versions of the Septuagint. For "hypocrite" meaning "transgressor," see Job 20:5 in Aquila's version. For the meaning "lawless," see Isa. 9:16 in Aquila's, Symmachus's, and Theodotion's versions; cf. Matt. 23:28.

5. This translation is a slightly modified version of the one in Betz's *Sermon on the Mount*, 199.

6. The *Didache*, a first-century church manual, refers to the position of the disciples as one of powerlessness. Following Jesus' recommendation not to demand back something forcibly taken, *Didache* 1.4 adds "for neither are you able." See Kirsopp Lake, *The Apostolic Fathers with an English Translation*, Loeb Classical Library (Cambridge, Mass.: Harvard University Press, 1977), 310–11.

7. Betz, *Sermon on the Mount*, 280.

8. This law stipulated that the closest male relative must take a widow and raise up children to carry on the name of her deceased husband. This relative was usually the brother of the deceased and the brother-in-law of the widow.

CHAPTER 5

The Psychology and Theology
of Confrontation

~

B EFORE PROCEEDING with the focus of this chapter, it may be helpful for the reader to review the movements in the forgiveness exchange as summarized in figures 1 and 2 on pp. 3 and 5. The last chapter investigated biblical texts dealing with confrontation. This investigation illuminated the understanding and practice of confrontation in the earliest Christian communities. Since confrontation is biblically sanctioned, the long-standing cultural aversion to face one another with the emotionally painful dimensions of relationships is surprising. This chapter explores the role of positive and painful emotions in healthy, life-giving relationships with attention to the need for a revaluation of human emotions. Central to this chapter is the identification of confrontation as key to interpersonal social growth and healing. Confrontation is explored as a form of *accurate empathic action*.

THE DEVALUING AND REVALUING OF HUMAN EMOTIONS

The cultural history of Western Christianity reveals that the ancient philosophical scheme depicted in figure 3 (see p. 53) continues to have an impact on the way modern people think and feel about their intrapsychic, interpersonal, and social lives. This mental framework and philosophical foundation are known as dualism. Without oversimplifying this complex scheme, the reader is invited to see how the illustration in figure 3 places various human realities and characteristics in opposition. The left column represents the place of privilege, and the right column lists those realities of lesser value. An innate hostility exists in dualism between the opposites and creates an almost Jekyll-and-Hyde dynamic in human experience.

One of the consequences of dualism is the belief that to be a truly holy or spiritual person, one must repress one's emotions and bodily passions. Emotions are hostile to reason and, if not controlled, result in irrational and dangerous behavior.[1] Emotions, especially the wild emotion of anger, must be tamed through the exercise of rationality. How often has it been said that "she is just too emotional to handle the situation" or "he has to learn to toughen up; crying at his age will be trouble" or "he was in a fit of rage and cannot be held responsible for his actions" or "she lets her feelings get in the way of making the hard decisions." The remnants of dualism teach moderns that emotions are gender specific and that the painful emotions of anger, shame, and guilt are almost beyond our control and must be suppressed and mastered to help us function intrapsychically, interpersonally, and socially. Repressing these painful emotions, however, is precisely one of the reasons why authentic engagement in the processes of forgiveness, repentance, and reconciliation eludes so many people.

> *One of the consequences of dualism is the belief that to be a truly holy or spiritual person, one must repress one's emotions and bodily passions.*

Feelings are essential in helping humans evaluate what is happening, and they deserve respect for what they are. Taking responsibility for positive and painful feelings enables persons to experience greater authenticity in relationships. Some contemporary Christian theologians have joined the endeavor to reconnect the body–mind split and to address the theological distortions of dualism.

FROM A CULTURE OF AVOIDANCE AND ALIENATION TO A CULTURE OF EMBRACE AND EMPATHY

A dualistic framework once assisted an emerging Western culture in making sense of reality. It was not until the time of the great philosopher Aristotle (384–322 B.C.E.) that the realities identified in

Figure 3
Philosophical Scheme of Dualism

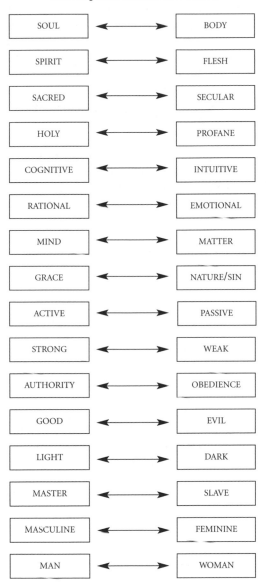

SOUL	BODY
SPIRIT	FLESH
SACRED	SECULAR
HOLY	PROFANE
COGNITIVE	INTUITIVE
RATIONAL	EMOTIONAL
MIND	MATTER
GRACE	NATURE/SIN
ACTIVE	PASSIVE
STRONG	WEAK
AUTHORITY	OBEDIENCE
GOOD	EVIL
LIGHT	DARK
MASTER	SLAVE
MASCULINE	FEMININE
MAN	WOMAN

figure 3 were understood as being in hostile opposition to one another.[2] Over time the acceptance of this mental framework left Western culture with a disdain for the affective dimension of the human personality. We see the affective dimension portrayed in media as almost always out of control, violent, demeaning, and exploitative. Culture stereotypes men into erroneously thinking that if forceful and painful emotions are not controlled, avoided, or consciously repressed, they inevitably will be led into acts of inhumanity, rage, and physical violence. Culture stereotypes women into erroneously thinking that if forceful and painful emotions are not controlled, avoided, or consciously repressed, they inevitably will be led to depression, manipulative behavior, and other forms of emotional violence. Women who act out violence are considered far more outrageous, socially unacceptable, and unnatural than men who engage in similar destructive behaviors. For example, it is common to devalue and disparage women's anger as hysterical and to value angered expression by men as righteously indignant.

A process of revaluing the role of both the positive and painful emotions in the lives of men and women who seek to discover more depth and authenticity in their relationships is under way in American Christian culture. This revaluing process directly impacts those who have been injured in a relationship and realize that their painful feelings are valuable sources of information and action. Those who hurt another either intentionally or unintentionally possess the prerogative to explore their own internal motivations when confronted with the offense. The emergence of a more integrated vision of the human person also considers the role religious faith plays in the experience of physical and mental health.

American culture often suggests that those who are suffering need only anesthetize the pain. This culture is indeed a pain-avoiding culture. Advances of modern medicine are certainly beneficial. Those who previously suffered terrible burdens of physical and emotional pain now have access to medications that assist them in living fuller and healthier lives. Those who need such chemical assistance to live more pain-free ought to do so with gratitude for the benefits of medical science. At the same time, however, abuses of drugs and misuses of alcohol and other substances prevent people from living healthy and responsible lives. Americans live within an addictive society that seduces with the slogan that there ought to be no pain in living and that disturbing personal, interpersonal, and social issues can be settled by sedation from the full freight of painful challenges. This lie of modern culture collides with the truth of the Christian message.

Even though it is influenced by a dualistic philosophy, the Christian religion embraces a theology and practice that are incarnational. God's decision to take on human flesh and blood, body and emotions, means that every aspect of the human person is sacred. While there is in human living the inevitability of sin, estrangement, and betrayal, grace can prevent these realities from distorting our beauty and possibility. Christians have access to living traditions that provide the encouragement and guidance of the biblical witness, the message of the Gospels, methods of personal prayer, regularity of communal worship, and a sacramental system rooted in the transforming power of grace. While all Christian sacraments bring the healing love of God in Christ, the postbaptismal sacraments of Reconciliation and the Anointing of the Sick celebrated in the Roman Catholic Church are particular moments of healing. Sacraments offer a healing alternative to avoidance and alienation. By using symbols arising from culture itself—bread, wine, oil, water, human presence, voice, and touch—the empathic relationship ignited by the sacramental moment conveys the actual and active presence of Christ's dispensing compassion and communion. Not haphazardly, Cardinal Bernardin and Steven Cook celebrated the Eucharist together following their confrontation and mutual exchange of forgiveness.

> *God's decision to take on human flesh and blood, body and emotions, means that every aspect of the human person is sacred.*

The desire to be a whole human being requires a person consciously to engage in the delicate balance of all aspects of being human—physical, emotional, mental, and spiritual. The debilitation of one aspect of our humanity impacts the whole of ourselves and our relational world. For example, emerging evidence-based research is finding that those individuals who remain filled with revenge toward other persons are less physically healthy than those who have negotiated some kind of forgiveness. Empirical studies now reveal that those who hold a religious commitment and are involved in a faith community are less likely to suffer from depression, cardiovascular disease, and immune system dysfunction. Such persons also experience fewer hospitalizations than those who lack a sense of intrinsic faith and who belong to a worship community.[3] Only within the past few years has it become more generally known and increasingly accepted that religious beliefs and practices impact physical and mental well-being.

Some religious beliefs and practices, however, can negatively affect living. Faith convictions and practices that are intellectually and emotionally repressive and controlling can result in a personal and relationally unproductive self-righteousness. A religion that instills fear, fosters compulsive behaviors, or leads to closed-mindedness, prejudice, and lack of human compassion toward others is the faith of neither Jesus Christ and his disciples nor that of the Christian church.

PAINFUL EMOTIONS AND THE POWER OF LOVE

Recent research conducted by psychologist David G. Myers reveals a somewhat grim picture of the lack of emotional/spiritual well-being among Americans. In the last half of the twentieth century, America has experienced an increased stress on individualism and individual rights. Such exclusive valuation placed on the individual has contributed to isolationism and flight from community. Where once the front porch was a welcome sign and gathering place for neighbors to pause and connect, most suburban homes now build a backyard deck securely fenced in for exclusive access. Individual control, personal security, and fear of litigation prompt a decline in altruism and the value of community. The overvaluation of individualism and a false sense of independence have resulted in an increase in depression, violence, suicide, divorce, and child neglect. American society covets wealth and materialism as essential values for the good life with the concomitant neglect of communitarian values, social ideals, and stewardship of the earth. The challenges and rewards of mutuality-based Christian community are easily misplaced within such a fractured context of contemporary living.

One response to restoring fractured well-being is the reintroduction of the value of spirituality and the faith factor in finding meaning and integration in daily living. The research done by Myers suggests that the integrated life of personal, interpersonal, and social well-being is available to all persons irrespective of gender, age, or race. Happiness is greater among those who are invested in close, supportive relationships and are able to bring to these relationships trust, optimism, and a healthy sense of self. Intrinsic faith, active religious commitment, focus beyond self, altruistic concerns, and a sense of meaning and purpose in life enhance a person's quality of life.[4] The grim picture of the disintegrative characteristics of America is countered by the knowledge that persons experience themselves as possessing inherent dignity and are capable of meaningful relationships. Human beings have the experience of knowing they are capable of transcending self-preoccupation and contribute to the concerns of other humans and creation itself. Therefore, the capacity to take one another seriously enough to confront one another with painful emotions is an authentic human capacity and relational expectation.

Ten years ago, Protestant theologian Beverly Wildung Harrison wrote an article entitled "The Power of Anger in the Work of Love." It was her conviction that society was neglecting the most human and most valuable and most central of all the works of love—the work of human communication, of caring and nurturance, and of tending the interpersonal bonds of true community.[5] Harrison believed it was essential to consider the relation of acts of love to anger:

> It is my thesis that we Christians have come very close to killing love precisely because we have understood anger to be a deadly sin. Anger is not the opposite of love. It is better understood as a feeling-signal that all is not well in our relation to other persons or groups or to the world around us. Anger is a mode of connectedness to others and it is always a vivid form of caring. To put the point another way: anger is—and it always is—a sign of some resistance in ourselves to the moral quality of the social relations in which we are immersed. To grasp this point—that anger signals something amiss in relationship—is a critical first step in understanding the power of anger in the work of love.[6]

Neither anger nor any other feeling automatically leads to wise and compassionate action. Also, painful feelings do not necessarily lead to violent and inhumane behavior. Instead, the painful feelings in life challenge the person to process the feeling more maturely into humane and just action. Both positive and negative feelings are ingredients in relational transactions. The avoidance of painful feelings such as anger continues to devalue an important resource in healing broken relationships.

> *"Anger is not the opposite of love. It is better understood as a feeling-signal that all is not well in our relation to other persons or groups or to the world around us."*

Harrison has reminded the Christian community that escapism and fear of feeling lead only to the stopgap measure of evasion. Evading the painful dimensions of interpersonal life will only lead to the accumulation of unfinished business and does not result in true healing. Avoiding and evading the pressure of painful feelings within relationships of consequence subvert the very desire to remain in relationship with those who, because we care about them, can hurt us the most. Harrison said it clearly: "Anger expressed directly is a mode of taking the other seriously, of caring. The important point is that where feeling is evaded, where anger is hidden or goes unattended . . . there the power of love . . . atrophies and dies."[7]

CONFRONTATION AS ACCURATE EMPATHIC ACTION

Confrontation in the interpersonal context is the direct bringing forward of painful subject matter. Unfortunately, many have perceived or experienced this form of human interaction as aggressive, emotionally violent, devoid of compassion, uncharitable, and even un-Christian. Embedded in dictionary definitions are references to confrontation such as "to present with contradictions, to acknowledge face to face, and to bring together for examination."[8] These understandings of confrontation are too often overlooked. The more pejorative popular notions prevail, insisting that confrontation is about the strong overpowering the weak and the active one dominating the passive, helpless victim. In the current American "golden age of lying," the skill of confrontation is a needed remedy for the obfuscation, deceit, fibs, and falsehoods that have become a well-honed art form. Far from being an intrusive maneuver, reclaiming confrontation in the commitment to authentic interpersonal life may in actuality be one of America's best hopes. In reality, confrontation is about sharing painful feelings with attention to oneself as confronter and with attention to the other who is receiving the message. Empathy is about being able to feel with another without losing a sense of one's own internal climate. Being empathic is a relational moment in which one person makes an authentic felt connection with another. The experience of empathy means that one is actually feeling with the other and aware that the emotion arises from within and is being shared interpersonally.

Confrontation as accurate empathic action requires that the confronter be ready to express the concern with the simultaneous ability to be attentive to the effect the confrontation may have on the one confronted. While confrontation holds the possibility of the rewards of deeper authenticity and health in a relationship of consequence, the moment of confrontation holds dangers for the confronter. There ought be no naiveté in the choice to confront. The confronter must have an accurate sense of the relational situation facing her or him and be sincerely ready to offer an empathic action to the perpetrator of the pain. Confrontation makes the confronter vulnerable again to the hurtful moment and to the possibility of feelings of anger, shame, ridicule, or rejection that may follow from threatening the offender's honor, dignity, or need for self-protection at all costs. The personal readiness of the confronter is essential, and she or he must have an accurate reading of the readiness of the offender to be confronted with the meaning of the offense. The promises and problems of accurate empathic action are abundant. There is no doubt that confrontation is a challenging dimension of interpersonal relationships.

> *Confrontation as accurate empathic action requires that the confronter be ready to express the concern with the simultaneous ability to be attentive to the effect the confrontation may have on the one confronted.*

The nature of interpersonal living means human beings interact in an intricate and intimate web of relationships. Human beings grow and develop interdependently. They exist and develop in a web of caring and challenging relationships and life experiences. The give and take, ebb and flow of caring are what make spending time with those of consequence a meaningful and nurturing activity. In authentic relationships humans take care of their emotional business, relate honestly, desire to develop stronger and more tender bonds of love, compromise to meet one another's sometimes competing needs, and learn to express and receive forgiveness. Because the bonds between humans are so essential and fragile, they often fear rejection by those who know them the best and longest and those who are most needed. The inevitability of the unexpected in relationships, including betrayal and undeserved hurt, throw people off balance and challenge even the most solid of relationships. Hurting relationships need rebalancing.

> *"Like Jesus, we are called to a radical activity of love, to a way of being in the world that deepens relation, embodies and extends community, passes on the gift of life."*

Rebalancing or restoring mutuality in relationships will not be possible without the art form of confrontation as accurate empathic action. Confrontation is a constituent part of love. It is a gospel value and a central virtue practiced by Jesus. "Like Jesus," Beverly Harrison said, "we are called to a radical activity of love, to a way of being in the world that deepens relation, embodies and extends community, passes on the gift of life."[9] Jesus calls human beings to confront that which has twisted and distorted the mutual love and trust between them. The path of confrontation includes empathic attention to one another, telling the truth of our experience without fear, and naming the wounding experience caused by another. A successful confrontation affirms that the other does indeed care enough about the interpersonal bond that he or she will, in turn, risk listening and engaging in the pain and anger for the sake of the love. If the desire to set the relationship right is authentic, then the act of coming into the presence of the other, wounded as one may be, holds the power and the grace to effect the desired change. *Confrontation need not and is not intended to be abusively confrontational. Accurate empathic action is essentially a respectful conversation. It is overcoming fear or any form of retribution to speak the truth in love.* To lose the power of confrontation and to extinguish this capacity from the repertoire of human relations are to miss the chance at the best of authentic relational harmony. Thus, confrontation as a relational skill must remain within the realm of possibility for most people.

Confrontation is an "art form" and a human relationship skill. Hopefully, you have a clear sense that striving to live and love authentically will inevitably include the need to confront another in a relationship of consequence. Fearing all forms of confrontation as interference and aggression serves only to deepen relational rifts, not heal them. Confrontation is a skill that must be embraced to live more honestly in freely chosen partnerships of love and trust. Sincere and well-prepared acts of confrontation hold the possibility of setting the stage and creating the condition for *metanoia*—a change of attitude, understanding, and heart. This change is essential to the process of forgiveness. Use the following Guide to Effective Confrontation to assist you in developing the "art form" of confrontation.

A GUIDE TO EFFECTIVE CONFRONTATION

Confrontation as Accurate Empathic Action

Confrontation is the capacity to take one another seriously enough to come into each other's presence as wounded and wounder. Confrontation involves a mutual facing into painful emotions because of the love and the desire not to lose the relationship to the fracture forever. Confrontation in interpersonal relationships of consequence assumes that the hurt does not necessarily have to be the final word in a relationship once experienced in confidence and trust.

The following information and series of self-reflective questions will assist the reader in preparing to engage the art form, virtue, and spiritual intelligence known as confrontation.

What Does It Mean to Be Accurate?

If the relationship is to be one of consequence, being accurate requires situating the hurt within that relationship. Being accurate means carefully assessing what actually happened to avoid exaggeration, distortion, and false perceptions of the facts.

◆ Have I completed my emotional and spiritual homework (intrapsychic) by carefully and critically exploring what happened in the fracturing moment? Have I explored the memory with as much honesty as I can muster?

◆ Have I named and owned the full range of emotions associated with the event and the offending person?

◆ Have I spent sufficient time with those painful emotions to understand their power and impact on me and in the relationship?

◆ Have I permitted myself and then worked through intense anger and the desire for revenge or retribution?

◆ Am I confident that I have moved into and beyond self-righteousness and moral superiority?

◆ Am I aware if this fracture has reinforced a sense of myself as victimized once again? If so, am I willing to explore my sense of victimization in order to prevent the possibility of becoming entrenched in self-pity or mired in self-justification?

◆ Have I a confidant, counselor, clergyperson, or spiritual companion whom I can ask for help in working through my painful feelings for the purpose of personal and interpersonal healing? Can I trust my own intrapsychic processes? Am I willing to open my introspection to a trusted other? Do I have the critical judgment and humility to ask for help in order to make sure I am "on the mark" when I have suffered from someone else's "missing the mark" with me?

◆ Am I recovering the desire to heal with the offending person by reflecting on the loving aspects of the history of the relationship and the innate worthiness of the person who wounded me?

◆ Have I found within myself and proceeded to explore what may have motivated the hurtful behavior of the offender?

◆ In carefully analyzing the possible motives of the offender have I uncovered mitigating circumstances or new information that may have prompted the offending behavior? If so, is it more appropriate to exonerate the person than to forgive the offender? In exoneration there is no need for forgiveness (see chapter 2).

+ Through the process of placing the hurt in a new context of critical self-reflection, have I recovered an empathic bond with the offender, thereby sensing within myself an openness to reconnect with the offender in order to express the pain for the purpose of shared healing and hope of repentance, forgiveness, and reconciliation?

+ Have I spent the time necessary to accurately read myself and appropriately ready myself to encounter the offender?

What Does Empathy Mean in This Context?

In the context of mutual encounter, empathy means that I am in touch with the range of my painful feelings, can articulate them in an appropriate manner, and at the same time, attend to the other person. If I feel no empathy for the other, I SHOULD NOT ACT at this time. If I cannot uncover and discover some empathic connection with the offender, it is not the time to take direct action to face the offender.

+ Am I able to enter a tense moment aware of my inner climate, to speak the truth in love (which includes the range of painful emotions, including anger), and simultaneously be aware of the impact of my sharing on the other? This is part of the art form of confrontation.

+ Am I ready to give myself to creating an interpersonal climate whereby the other can hear me, understand me (an occasion of *metanoia*), and be given space to respond to me (an occasion of repentance)?

+ Have I considered the outcome should the offender repent? Am I aware of what I need from the other in terms of new behavior in order for me to assess that the repentance is authentic? If I assess the apology as genuine, am I prepared to invest in a reconciled relationship experienced in *new time*?

+ Have I considered what the relationship could be and become in the new time of reconciliation? Since reconciliation is experienced on a continuum, do I have a sense of my expectations for the future?

+ Will the gesture of forgiveness given and received be a closure to the relationship because, while the rupture has been forgiven, there is no hope for future restoration? Am I prepared to accept this reality and/or share that information with the repentant offender?

What Does Action Mean?

Longing for the experience of the giving and receiving of forgiveness can lead to action when the fear of acting is overcome by the careful and prayerful preparation to actually encounter the other in an interpersonal engagement called confrontation. All the intrapsychic work moves in the direction of the graced human capacity to take seriously the profound and fragile bonds between people and to risk acting with courage and compassion to restore love torn asunder.

- What am I doing to read the situation of the other person in order to assess the timing of my honest and caring encounter with her or him?

- Have I been clear with the offender that the invitation to meet is specifically to explore the rupture experienced in the relationship?

- Is my invitation expressed in language and tone that disclose a genuine interest in authentic mutual dialogue?

- Have we mutually agreed upon a time and place that allow for sufficient privacy and appropriate length of time for the conversation?

- Am I prepared for the possibility that the action of the encounter could be a re-wounding experience or that I might hear something unexpected about my own complicity in causing the rupture?

- Am I secure enough in my own preparation to know when and if the dialogue needs to be concluded to protect myself from any form of revictimization?

What to Do When Direct Accurate Empathic Action Is Impossible?

If interpersonal confrontation is not possible and may be physically or psychically dangerous, the skills of transferring the offender to God may be ritualized to assist the injured person in becoming free of the responsibility for forgiveness (see chapters 8–9).

NOTES

1. For a contemporary and pastoral approach to emotions as allies in spiritual growth, see James D. Whitehead and Evelyn Eaton Whitehead, *Shadows of the Heart: A Spirituality of the Painful Emotions* (New York: Crossroad, 1994).

2. For a detailed history of the philosophy of dualism and its impact on male and female, masculine and feminine development, see Prudence Allen, *The Concept of Woman: The Aristotelian Revolution, 750 B.C.–A.D. 1250* (Montreal: Eden Press, 1985).

3. See Harold Koenig, *The Healing Power of Faith* (New York: Simon & Schuster, 1999); idem, *Religion and Health* (New York: Oxford University Press, 2000).

4. See David G. Myers, *The Pursuit of Happiness: Who Is Happy—and Why* (New York: Avon, 1992); idem, "Close Relationships and Quality of Life," in *Foundations of Hedonic Psychology: Scientific Perspectives on Enjoyment and Suffering,* ed. D. Kahnerman, E. Diener, and N. Schwarz (New York: Russell Sage Foundation, forthcoming).

5. Beverly Wildung Harrison, "The Power of Anger in the Work of Love," in *Weaving the Vision,* ed. Judith Plaskow and Carol Christ (San Francisco: Harper & Row, 1989), 203.

6. Ibid., 206.

7. Ibid., 207.

8. *The Random House College Dictionary* (New York: Random House, 1992).

9. Harrison, "Power of Anger," 210.

CHAPTER 6

Biblical Insights into
Repentance and Accountability

∾

T HE FIRST STEP in the forgiveness exchange is confrontation, and the second is repentance, which follows as the appropriate response to confrontation. The offended confronts; the offender repents. Confrontation is the responsibility of the offended; repentance is the responsibility of the offender. The offended most often initiates confrontation; the offender responds by repenting. Repentance enables the offended to *offer* forgiveness, and the offender to *receive* this forgiveness. Repentance is therefore a necessary step in the forgiveness exchange.

REPENTANCE, A PREREQUISITE FOR FORGIVENESS

The New Testament insists that genuine repentance is a necessary prerequisite for forgiveness. Jesus prescribes forgiveness for a repentant sinner (Matt. 18:15c), but expulsion and not forgiveness for a recalcitrant transgressor (Matt. 18:16–17). Jesus then bequeaths to his church the authority and responsibility not to forgive the unrepentant (i.e., "to bind") as well as to forgive the repentant (i.e., "to loose") (Matt. 18:18).

> *"I say to you, not seven times but seventy-times seven."*
> *(Matt. 18:21–22)*

Peter's follow-up question to Jesus' prescription elicits a response from Jesus that on the surface appears to demand forgiveness without repentance. Peter inquires how often he should forgive a brother who sins against him (Matt. 18:21). Jesus responds, "I say to you, not seven times but seventy-times seven" (Matt. 18:21–22). Jesus' response seems to support the adage to simply forgive the wrongdoer and forget the misdeed. The parable of the Unforgiving Servant that immediately follows this exchange between Jesus and Peter in Matthew's Gospel, however, emphasizes the necessity of genuine repentance before forgiveness is extended.

In this familiar parable, Jesus tells of a debtor who owes his master ten thousand talents, which Jesus describes as "a huge amount" (Matt. 18:24). Actually, a talent represents six thousand drachmas, and a single drachma is a customary day's wage for workers. This debtor is sixty million days' wages in debt. Jesus' understatement that "he had no way of paying it back" (Matt. 18:25) probably brings a smile to his audience. This smile likely yields to a burst of laughter when this debtor implores his master, "Be patient with me, and I will pay you back in full" (Matt. 18:26). The posture of this debtor in falling down and doing homage to his master (Matt. 18:26) as well as his words of admission that he is indeed responsible for the debt elicits compassion from this master, who immediately forgives the entire amount! Later, however, this "forgiven" debtor finds another who owes him one hundred days' wages or drachmas and demands that he pay up (Matt. 18:28). Disregarding this person's entreaty for leniency, the "forgiven" debtor delivers him over to prison (Matt. 18:30). These actions demonstrate to the master that the "forgiven" debtor's posture and words did not represent genuine repentance. Consequently, the master recalls the "forgiven" debtor and reinstates the entire original debt (Matt. 18:34).

Jesus' parable demonstrates that *genuine* repentance is absolutely necessary for forgiveness. Even in a case where forgiveness is already extended, forgiveness may be revoked if the injured party discovers that the transgressor only made a show of repentance. Thus, this parable of the Unforgiving Servant indicates that repentance is a prerequisite for the forgiveness enjoined upon Peter by Jesus' response to Peter's inquiry about how often he should forgive an offender.

> *The New Testament insists that genuine repentance is a necessary prerequisite for forgiveness.*

In addition to this parable, other New Testament passages such as Colossians 3:13 and Ephesians 4:32 advocate genuine repentance as a necessary prerequisite for forgiveness. In both these passages, the Lord's forgiveness serves as the paradigm for his followers' forgiveness. Colossians 3:13b reads, "As the Lord has forgiven you, so must you also do." Ephesians 4:32b reads, "Forgiving one another as God has forgiven you in Christ." Throughout the New Testament, the announcement of God's forgiveness is preceded by a call for repentance. According to the author of Acts, Peter instructs the crowds on the Day of Pentecost, "Repent and be baptized, every one of you, in the name of Jesus Christ for the forgiveness of your sins" (Acts 2:38). This author also presents Paul as summarizing his message before King Agrippa by saying, "I preached the need to repent and turn to God, and to do works giving evidence of repentance" (Acts 26:20). If a sinner's repentance is a prerequisite for the Lord's extending forgiveness and the Lord's forgiveness is a paradigm for Christian forgiveness, then genuine repentance is also a necessary prerequisite for the forgiveness of a transgressor.

REPENTANCE, A CHANGED UNDERSTANDING

The necessity of repentance in the forgiveness exchange emphasizes the need for offenders to repent genuinely and for those offended to recognize genuine repentance. All of us fail and are failed at one time or another and experience ourselves as both offender and offended. When we offend, we usually feel the need to repent but are frequently unclear about how to proceed or what to do. When we are offended, we sometimes receive an apology, but often wonder whether the apology was really sincere or merely contrived. Our need both to repent and to recognize genuine repentance requires us to understand the true nature of repentance.

In the New Testament, the English word *repentance* translates the Greek word μετάνοια (*metanoia*), which means to change one's understanding. Repentance is the change in the offender's understanding of the words or actions that caused the offense. This change in understanding enables us as offenders to own our responsibility in causing the offense and to alter our future behavior so that the offense is less likely to be repeated. Our repentance thus gives those we offend some assurance that they will not likely be hurt again in the same way. Those we offend can extend forgiveness to us as repentant offenders and treat our offensive act as resolved because we have owned our responsibility for the offense and recognized the right of those we offended not to be hurt in this manner again.

> *Repentance is the change in the offender's understanding of the words or actions that caused the offense.*

Several biblical examples illustrate this conception of repentance as a change of understanding. Before Jesus confronts Saul, alias Paul, on the Damascus road, Paul is vigorously opposing the followers of Jesus. According to Acts, Paul is "breathing murderous threats against the disciples of the Lord" (Acts 9:1) and traveling to Damascus to seek "men and women who belonged to the Way" that "he might bring them back to Jerusalem in chains" (Acts 9:2). Saul views his opposition as progression in Judaism and as zeal for his ancestral traditions, which he feels the followers of Jesus threaten (Gal. 1:13–17; cf. Acts 22:3–5; 26:9–11). He considers himself neither a murderer nor a persecutor but a zealot for the laws of God.

Following his encounter with Jesus on the Damascus road, however, Paul changes his understanding of his actions. For three days, he prays and fasts. Then "things like scales [fall] from his eyes and he [regains] his sight" (Acts 9:18). These scales metaphorically describe his change in understanding. After this encounter, Paul describes his former actions as persecuting the church of God beyond measure and trying to destroy it (Gal. 1:13). He feels unworthy to be an apostle because of his former acts of persecution (1 Cor. 15:9). Instead of zealous service to God, Paul now understands his actions as murder and as fighting against God. This change of understanding is the essence of Paul's repentance.

Paul's genuine repentance alters his conduct and his relationship with those he formerly offended. He ceases his persecution of the disciples of Jesus and becomes one himself. As a follower of Jesus, Paul now suffers persecution and proclaims the faith in Jesus that he had formerly tried to destroy (Gal. 1:23). Paul's genuine repentance enables those he formerly persecuted to extend forgiveness and Paul himself to receive this forgiveness. Paul is forgiven not only by Jesus but also by those whom he had once persecuted, and they now glorify God because of him (Gal. 1:22–24). Paul's acceptance in the Christian community in Jerusalem demonstrates the effectiveness of his repentance in altering his conduct and his relationship with those he had formerly offended.

In addition to Paul, Zacchaeus the tax collector also illustrates repentance as a change of understanding. The Gospel of Luke describes Zacchaeus as a "chief tax collector" and a "wealthy man" (19:2). Indeed, tax collectors in the Roman empire usually acquired wealth. Such individuals purchased the right to collect taxes by paying the entire yearly tax sum in advance to the appropriate authorities. The tax collectors were then authorized to assess taxes on goods and services in their area of jurisdiction. Collecting more during the year than they paid at the beginning of the year represented their profit. Such a system encouraged the collection of more taxes than were needed and was rife with abuse. When tax collectors come to John the Baptist, he admonishes them by saying, "Stop collecting more than what is prescribed" (Luke 3:13). As a "chief tax collector," Zacchaeus had ample opportunities for personal gain and was undoubtedly a "wealthy man."

Having official authorization to collect taxes, Zacchaeus could consider his conduct justified. His fellow citizens, however, did not. The crowd in Jericho consider him a sinner (Luke 19:7), and Jesus describes him as lost (Luke 19:10). Confronted with the presence of Jesus, Zacchaeus repents. He changes his understanding of his conduct and the wealth he has taken from others. He states, "Behold, half of my possessions, Lord, I shall give to the poor, and if I have extorted anything from anyone I shall repay it four times over" (Luke 19:8). Zacchaeus demonstrates the genuineness of his repentance by transcending the requirements of the law. Numbers 5:6–7 stipulates, "If a man [or a woman] commits a fault against his fellow man and wrongs him . . . he shall confess the wrong he has done, restore his ill-gotten goods in full, and in addition give one-fifth of their value to the one he has wronged." Instead of only one-fifth, Zacchaeus offers fourfold restitution. His genuine repentance elicits Jesus' swift response, "Today salvation has come to this house." Jesus includes Zacchaeus in the family of Abraham (Luke 19:9) and in the community of the saved (19:10).

Zacchaeus's changed understanding of his former conduct enables Jesus to extend forgiveness and Zacchaeus to receive this forgiveness.

Not only Paul and Zacchaeus but also David illustrates repentance as a change of understanding. David's sordid affair with Bathsheba is well known. He first sees her from a distance as he walks around on the roof of his palace and as she bathes in her private courtyard. He is immediately attracted to this beautiful woman and makes inquiries about her. He is told, "She is Bathsheba, daughter of Eliam, and wife of Uriah the Hittite" (1 Sam. 11:3). To this point, David has not sinned, for the attraction of human sexuality is God-given. As soon as he learns that she is the wife of Uriah, David should cease pursuing her. According to God's law, she is off limits to him. David does not desist, however, but invites her to his palace, where he seduces her. He uses his God-given elevated status of power, privilege, and prestige to invade her privacy and then her morality. He makes her an adulteress by becoming an adulterer himself.

David is now caught in the web of sin, and its strands begin to confine him and ensnare him more completely. Bathsheba communicates to David the three most feared words for any man who has violated another man's wife. "I am pregnant," she says. Fulfilling his duties in David's army, her husband Uriah has been away for some time, and her pregnancy is a clear sign of her unfaithfulness to him. Both she and David, her adulterer, are liable to the death penalty (Lev. 20:10; Deut. 22:22). David is caught in the web of sin that threatens to destroy his power, privilege, prestige, and even his own life.

Acting swiftly, he summons Uriah from the battlefield under the pretext of receiving a report from him. David's real intent is to deceive Uriah into thinking that David's child is his own. He dismisses Uriah with the command, "Go down to your house and bathe your feet" (2 Sam. 11:8). Even though the bathing of the feet is a common custom after a journey, David's sin perverts the meaning of his command. The term *feet* is often used as a euphemism for the genitals (Judg. 3:24; Ruth 3:4, 8, 14; 2 Kgs. 18:27 *Qere;* Isa. 6:2; cf. Ezek. 16:25). David thus commands Uriah to go home and have sexual relations with his wife. Uriah's duty as a soldier prohibits sexual activity, which would render him unfit for military service, and so he sleeps in the military barracks (Deut. 23:10–12; 1 Sam. 21:5–6). The next day, he responds to David, "Can I go home to eat and to drink and to sleep with my wife? As the Lord lives and as you live, I will do no such

thing" (2 Sam. 11:11). David's attempt to cover his sin by treacher-
ously deceiving Uriah has failed because of Uriah's faithfulness and
loyalty to his military obligations.

Desperate, David devises a new strategy. He summons Uriah and
sends him back to the battlefield with a sealed message for the commander who is instructed to place Uriah at the head of the charge,
where he is sure "to be struck down dead" (2 Sam. 11:15). Unwittingly,
Uriah delivers his own death sentence. After the commander sends
word to David that Uriah has fallen in battle, David nonchalantly
responds, "The sword devours now here and now there" (2 Sam.
11:25). David's sin of adultery has now led him to murder Uriah.
David marries Bathsheba, who gives birth to a son. It appears that
David's strategy has worked and that his sins are covered.

> *David's repentance consists of his changed understanding
> of his sin.*

David's cover-up demonstrates that he considers his sin to be only
a human concern. Nevertheless, the Lord has seen what David has
done and is divinely concerned (2 Sam. 11:27). The Lord sends his
prophet Nathan to confront David. Nathan asks David, "Why have
you spurned the Lord and done evil in his sight?" Nathan then curtly
depicts David's sins by saying, "You have cut down Uriah the Hittite
with the sword; you took his wife as your own, and him you killed
with the sword" (2 Sam. 12:9). David's repentance is swift. "I have
sinned against the Lord," he says (2 Sam. 12:13). Nathan immediately
responds, "The Lord on his part has forgiven your sin: you shall not
die" (2 Sam. 12:13). When confronted by the Lord, David repents. Sat-
isfied with David's repentance, the Lord forgives. David's repentance
thus enables the Lord to forgive him and enables David to receive the
Lord's forgiveness.

In this story of David's sordid affair with Bathsheba, David's repentance consists of his changed understanding of his sin. Throughout
the story, David acts as though his sin is against one man. By killing
Uriah, David considers the affair resolved. After he is confronted,
however, David understands his sin as a sin against the Lord that
threatens not only himself but also his entire kingdom. Indeed, Gen-

esis 20:6 and 39:9 consider adultery to be a sin against God. The Psalmist expands upon David's confession in this story and emphasizes both the divine and the social dimensions of David's sin (Psalm 51). David petitions the Lord:

> Have mercy on me, God,
> in your goodness;
> in your abundant compassion
> blot out my offense.
> Wash away all my guilt;
> from my sin cleanse me.
> For I know my offense;
> my sin is always before me.
> Against you alone have I sinned;
> I have done such evil in your sight
> that you are just in your sentence,
> blameless when you condemn. (Ps. 51:3–6)

In this Psalm, David asks not only for personal healing but also for the healing of his society (51:15) and Jerusalem (51:20-21). David truly repents of his sin by changing his understanding of his actions.

> *Repentance gives the offended some assurance of not being harmed again and enables the offended to extend forgiveness to these repentant offenders.*

Paul, Zacchaeus, and David all illustrate repentance as a change of understanding. Following confrontation, each changes his conception of his former actions. Each owns his responsibility in causing offense to the confronter, and each alters his future behavior so that the offense is not repeated. In the case of each, repentance gives the offended some assurance of not being harmed again and enables the offended to extend forgiveness to these repentant offenders. It also enables the offended to treat the offensive act as resolved because these offenders own their responsibility for the offense and recognize the right of the offended not to be hurt in this manner again. Repentance enables Paul, Zacchaeus, and David to receive this forgiveness. Repentance as a change of understanding is thus a necessary step in the forgiveness exchange.

DISTINGUISHING GENUINE
FROM CONTRIVED REPENTANCE

Those of us involved in this exchange as the offended need to distinguish genuine repentance from other possible responses to confrontation, so that we will know when to extend forgiveness. Neither remorse nor regret (μεταμέλεια) is repentance (μετάνοια). Repentance focuses on the offensive deed and its impact on the offended, but remorse and regret focus on the perpetrator and the repercussions he or she may encounter. Repentance is a change of understanding about the deed, but remorse and regret simply describe an uncomfortable feeling about the deed.

Judas and Peter provide an excellent contrast between remorse and repentance. After betraying Jesus, Judas is filled with remorse (μεταμεληθείς) when he sees that Jesus is condemned (Matt. 27:3). He returns the thirty pieces of silver for which he had betrayed Jesus and then hangs himself (Matt. 27:5). He feels deep remorse but does not repent. He does not try to understand his conduct in such a way that the destructive consequences might be overcome and his relationship with Jesus might be restored. After denying Jesus, Peter weeps bitterly at the Roostercrow Watch of the night (Matt. 26:75; cf. Mark 13:35). In contrast to Judas, however, Peter understands his action as a fulfillment of "the word that Jesus had spoken" (Matt. 26:75). Peter repents, and his subsequent actions mitigate against the negative consequences of his conduct. Just as he denied Jesus three times, so he affirms his love for Jesus three times (John 21:15–20), and his relationship with Jesus is restored. Remorse and regret are feelings that may prompt those who harm us to a change of understanding, but these feelings alone are not repentance and do not result in a successful forgiveness exchange between ourselves and our offenders.

> *Repentance focuses on the offensive deed and its impact on the offended, but remorse and regret focus on the perpetrator and the repercussions he or she may encounter. Repentance is a change of understanding about the deed, but remorse and regret simply describe an uncomfortable feeling about the deed.*

Neither is rationalization repentance. Rationalization is an attempt to justify actions by an appeal to internal or external circumstances. It focuses on the offender and minimizes the offense. The perpetrator reasons that the way he or she is or the way the circumstances are explains and justifies the offensive action. Rationalization may enable us as the offended to exonerate our offender, but it does not enable us to forgive. When we perceive rationalization simply as a way for our offender to avoid responsibility, rationalization usually leads to increased anger toward the offender rather than forgiveness.

Saul provides a clear example of rationalization. After he is confronted by Samuel for inappropriately offering a sacrifice, Saul responds, "When I saw that the men were slipping away from me, since you had not come by the specified time . . . in my anxiety I offered up the holocaust" (1 Sam. 14:11–12). Saul does not repent but offers reasons to explain his offering of the sacrifice. After Saul is again disobedient in sparing the best spoils of a war in which he was instructed to destroy everything, Samuel again confronts Saul, who explains, "The men spared the best sheep and oxen to sacrifice to the Lord" (1 Sam. 15:15). Samuel responds that the Lord prefers obedience to sacrifice, and Saul's rationalization does not result in his forgiveness. Instead, he is rejected from being king. Compared to Saul, David's sins are far worse. Nevertheless, David repents and is forgiven; Saul rationalizes and is rejected. Rationalization is not repentance and does not result in a successful forgiveness exchange.

> *Rationalization is an attempt to justify actions by an appeal to internal or external circumstances. It focuses on the offender and minimizes the offense.*

Neither is reversal of the charge or shifting of blame repentance. Reversal of the charge ignores both the offense and the offender and focuses instead on the one confronting. By shifting blame, the offender identifies the confronter as the problem. This response to confrontation is as old as the first sin in the Garden of Eden. After God confronts Adam with his sin of eating the forbidden fruit, Adam retorts, "The woman *whom you put here with me*—she gave me fruit from the tree, and so I ate it" (Gen. 3:12). Adam lays the blame on God for giving him this woman, but Adam's shifting of blame does not release him from judgment (Gen. 3:17–19). Reversing the charge or shifting the blame is not repentance and does not enable the one wounded to extend forgiveness. These possible responses to confrontation are alternatives to genuine repentance but do not result in a successful forgiveness exchange.

> *Reversal of the charge ignores both the offense and the offender and focuses instead on the one confronting.*

APPLICATION

Repentance is a very different response to confrontation. It is a change of understanding that alters future conduct and is the appropriate response to confrontation in contrast to remorse, rationalization, or reversal of the charge. In repentance, offenders change their understanding of the offense, and the offended receive satisfaction that the offense will not likely happen again. By repentance, we restore the personhood of those we offend by owning responsibility for the offense and affirming their feelings of offense. Repentance both enables those of us who are offended to extend an offer of forgiveness and those of us who offend to receive this forgiveness. Following confrontation, repentance is an absolutely necessary step in the forgiveness exchange.

- How do you define repentance? How does your definition distinguish repentance from remorse, regret, rationalization, reversal of the charge, or shifting of blame?

- In the Bible, repentance most often means a change of understanding. How does this definition of repentance relate to your own definition?

- The Bible presents repentance as a necessary prerequisite for forgiveness. Do you agree or disagree?

- Have you ever owned your harmful behavior and experienced repentance as a real change of understanding in response to someone's confronting you? How did you feel? What effects did your repentance have on you and on the person who confronted you?

♦ Have you ever confronted someone and received genuine repentance as a response? In what ways did that repentance facilitate your extending the offer of forgiveness? In what ways did the offender's repentance facilitate her or his acceptance of your forgiveness?

♦ Reflect on the repentance of Paul, Zacchaeus, and David. With whom does your experience and understanding of repentance resonate?

♦ In your journal, narrate your experience of repentance in your relationship with God and at least one significant person in your life.

CHAPTER 7

Theological and Psychological
Insights into Repentance

⤳

THUS FAR IN THIS BOOK, we have rooted our understandings of
human personality and potentiality within a theological vision.
The Christian vision of the human person accepts the inescapably
social nature of human beings. Human striving is both graced and
flawed. Fractures in love and trust are interwoven into the fabric of
ordinary human interpersonal and social relationships. In a sense,
humans grow into maturity through successfully or unsuccessfully
negotiating the stagelike unfolding of human becoming. The conscious free exercise of decision and choice and the shaping influences
of culture, sociohistorical context, family, school, neighborhood,
church, media, and technology forge personality and individuality.
Humans possess a magnitude of freedom regarding human and spiritual growth and, at the same time, are conditioned by influences not
of their making and into which they are born. Theologically, human
beings possess, in Karl Rahner's terminology, the infinity of absolute
spiritual openness to becoming and, simultaneously, are conditioned
and constrained by the finitude of human frailty and fallenness.

The biblical, theological, and psychological basis laid thus far indicates that the capacity to engage in the forgiveness process is both a
realizable human potential and a Christian mandate. There is no
question that the process of forgiveness thrives within the desires of
actual forgiving personalities. Psychologist Dr. Robert Emmons says:

> Forgiveness can activate integrative tendencies in the person, rescuing
> the psyche from inner conflict and turmoil, transforming the person
> from a state of fragmentation to a state of integration, from separation
> to reconciliation. . . . Forgiveness research can demonstrate that the

healing effects of forgiveness extend beyond personal happiness, health, and well-being, to a deeper sense of coherence, wholeness, and integration of the self.[1]

The forgiving personality, then, is a maturely developed one in which repenting is a constituent element.

THE REPENTANCE-SENSITIVE PERSONALITY

The English word *repentance* derives from the French *repentir* and means "to be sorry for." Repentance is the attitude and action motivated by the desire to undo harm. To do penance or act in a penitent manner is not about self-punishment or the experience of some form of retribution. Repentance is a wholehearted acceptance of one's responsibility in harming another or others and the change in attitude and understanding that brings forth healing behaviors. Repentance and forgiveness form a cornerstone for the healing of emotional and relational wounds after transgression.

In Christian life and practice, forgiveness is intricately linked to repentance, and the ability to repent arises from the personality that has developed the capacity to abandon, when necessary, the egocentric position of always being right and needing everything and everyone to be an extension of one's own needs. Such a personality possesses several virtues conducive to repentance. These virtues include empathy in contrast to narcissistic self-absorption, humility in contrast to self-aggrandizement, gratitude in contrast to resentment, and largesse of mind and heart in contrast to self-protection and defensiveness.

> *Repentance is the attitude and action motivated by the desire to undo harm. In Christian life and practice, forgiveness is intricately linked to repentance.*

Each of these virtues is a facility, a disposition or attitude that moves one to accomplish a moral good even against obstacles and at the cost of personal sacrifice. Each is not only a cultivated moral habit or quality but also an inherent force within human beings that empowers them to act in truly *therapeutic* ways. The medieval Benedictine abbess and theologian Hildegard of Bingen (1098–1179), taught and wrote that virtues arise from the synergy of divine grace and human cooperation. Virtues are healing arts embedded within the spiritual capacities of God's creatures and have a therapeutic function in the interrelationship of humans with humans and all of creation. Virtues demonstrate what it means to take a stand and assume responsibility in any given situation. According to Hildegard, virtues are brought about in people by God. Thus, the virtues of empathy, humility, gratitude, and largesse of mind and heart provide venues for self-realization-in-relationship and, in a sense, for divinizing our humanity.[2]

> *Compassion means to feel with the suffering of another.*

The virtue of empathy has a passive counterpart in compassion. Compassion means to feel with the suffering of another. The Gospels often portray Jesus as looking with or having compassion on others. Literally, the Greek verb σπλαγχνίζεσθαι means "to be moved in one's bowels." Thus, a compassionate person is literally moved at the level of their deepest parts in response to another's pain or suffering. Whereas compassion is an immediate uncritical interior emotional movement, empathy is an active effort to critically understand another person's perceptions of an interpersonal event as if one were that other person, rather than judging the other person's behavior from the perspective of one's own experience of that event.[3] If the process of forgiveness requires both the offender and the offended to attempt to understand the motives arising in each other, then the capacity to adopt an empathic view toward each other is critical to repentance and forgiveness.

Humility is a virtue akin to truth. To be humble is neither to belittle oneself nor to hold oneself in low esteem or of little value. Quite the contrary, a humble person has a critically honest and self-loving appraisal of himself or herself and a sense of perspective and self-acceptance. Emmons reports, "Humility is the disposition to view oneself as basically equal with any other human being even if there are objective differences in physical beauty, wealth, social skills, intelligence or other resources."[4] Because one has nurtured the virtue of humility, one is able to accept her or his imperfections and weave them into the pattern of one's whole self. If repentance is the whole-hearted acceptance of complicity in hurting another, then humility is that therapeutic power that enables a person to gracefully submit to self-critical honesty in pursuit of loving one's neighbor as oneself. The empathic and truly humble person is able to dismiss any impulse to either superiority or inferiority, to dispel the entanglement of unhealthy guilt or shame, and to accept the possibility of having injured another, along with the desire to cooperate in the healing of the wound. Humility, like empathy, plays a vital role in exercising and engaging the call to repentance.

> *"Humility is the disposition to view oneself as basically equal with any other human being even if there are objective differences in physical beauty, wealth, social skills, intelligence or other resources."*

The repentance-sensitive personality is one that takes seriously the theological conviction that life is a gift. Even amid the tumult, uncertainty, pain, and undeserved suffering that come with living, the pervasive vision of life is one of "gratulation," a feeling of joy, pleasure, warmth, and appreciation for the unmerited gift of life. Gratitude is a subtle virtue in human personality. It is the relief upon which to see more clearly the other virtues that inspire and direct the action of repentance. Since life is given as gratis, it is meant to be lived thankfully. A sensitive demeanor marks the person who bears and nurtures the virtue of gratitude. Without the activation of this essential impulse and virtue in the human personality, the challenges of living and loving can become the seedbed for resentment, bitterness, and exaggerated self-entitlement. In the repentant and forgiving personality, gratitude arises from a spiritual center within the human personality that views life as a gift and the quest for love as a wonderfully human and graced adventure.

If humans are theologically and psychologically rooted in the soil of gratitude, the virtues of humility and empathy grow from seedlings to generous ways of being-in-relationship. Largesse of mind and heart is the by-product of such living. Largesse refers to a liberal generosity in the bestowal of gifts. The virtue of largesse is identical to the loving productivity of Erikson's seventh and eighth stages of psychosocial development, which result in ways of living expressed by generativity and integrity. Life-cycle development involves a movement of the self in time in which each season of life brings new challenges requiring adaptive growth and change. In this natural and graced process, the repertoire of a person's abilities and flexibility can increase to the point of largesse of mind and heart. It is the divine gift bound to the wearisome and rewarding struggle for the life-giving balance of cherishing oneself and giving oneself away in love. Because one holds sacred one's own dignity and nurtures the virtue of largesse, one is able to grant to others that same dignity. Such largesse is exhibited in an awareness of and an ability to act from internal freedom, lack of defensiveness, fearlessness, and courage. Qualities of playfulness, humor, and reverence arise from a love of life and a love for others that sees in them the promise of the persons God is calling them to be.[5]

> *In the forgiving and repenting personality, the individual possesses a well-developed inner life.*

In the forgiving and repenting personality, the individual possesses a well-developed inner life whereby he or she is able to regulate and negotiate the painful emotions that can lead to the nonconstructive expression of anger, unhealthy guilt, overbearing shame, destructive and debilitating ruminations, and seething unattended resentments. Critically and carefully negotiating the minefields of pessimism and cynicism allows for equal time to nurture and experience the gift of gratitude and a largesse of mind and heart. The development of the virtues of empathy, humility, gratitude, and interior largesse are components of what could be called "spiritual intelligence."[6] While humans negotiate the actions of repenting through psycho-emotional processes, repentance is a spiritually funded movement of the mind and heart, prompted and guided by human desire and God's unrelenting grace to make all things new.

PERSONALITY DEFICITS

While a certain degree of self-focus and self-regard is absolutely necessary in a fully functioning personality, recent research indicates that "the narcissistic personality has become the most prominent personality type today in the Western world."[7] The dominant worldview of the secular American culture overvalues personal and immediate gratification and a kind of individualism that magnifies a "normal" narcissism. Narcissistic dynamics are naturally present in life-cycle development. A healthy degree of self-concern, self-protection, and self-care is vital to ego development and the ability to engage constructively in the forgiveness exchange. In the psychology of forgiveness, *unhealthy* narcissism is emerging as a central organizing constraint that destroys the natural development of the virtues of empathy, humility, gratitude, and largesse of mind and heart. Emmons contends, "In fact, conceivably, there is no other personality constraint with greater relevance for forgiveness than narcissism."[8] Excessive self-preoccupation is an enemy of the forgiving personality. Repentance is simply much more difficult for those with significant deficits in emotional development and spiritual intelligence.

> *"There is no other personality constraint with greater relevance for forgiveness than narcissism."*

Narcissism is "self-admiration that is characterized by tendencies toward grandiose ideas, exhibitionism, and defensiveness in response to criticism; interpersonal relationships that are characterized by feelings of entitlement, exploitativeness, and lack of empathy."[9] Narcissistic persons possess a hypersensitivity to others' criticism, overreact to minor frustrations, maintain a sense of entitlement to special rights and privileges, whether warranted or not. They have a heightened sense of what is due them, lack interpersonal/social reciprocity and empathy, and tend toward a selfish spirit. Even while attracting others to cater to their needs, such individuals often carry a deep sense of unworthiness and emptiness. Suspicion abounds, trust decreases, anger escalates, and the self-protective armor shields the fear of vulnerability. Of course, the excessively self-absorbed person does not open herself or himself to explore the possibility that these character traits are impeding the quality of his or her life. Someone else must be to blame, for they experience themselves as always right.

Most often maintaining a self-perception of a victim, the narcissistic person expresses surprise and anger when others fail to provide what is due them.[10] The central issue for people with narcissistic preoccupation is the preservation of their *persona*—private and public image—not the quality of their relations with other people. At all cost, they must retain a favorable image of themselves against any threats to their ego. Such intrapsychic and interpersonal relational patterns result in an interpersonal exploitation due to the lack of capacity for close relationships and unresolved issues with trust. Often these individuals experience failure in the ability to express nurturance for others. They exhibit excessive dependence, lack of inner serenity, and an underdeveloped ability to read relational cues about the needs of others.[11] Since those with such character deficits do not respond to the healthy trigger mechanism of guilt, they simultaneously fail to see their need for forgiveness. Because they are prone more to shame than guilt, narcissistic persons fail to recognize the impact of their offending behavior on others. When confronted, they enter a state of threat and anger that leads to a "rigidity in relationships and the generation of hidden agendas."[12]

Genuine repentance eludes the self-preoccupied personality. Repentance requires an interior mental and spiritual openness to be self-critical and nondefensive enough to accept the possibility of having caused harm to another. As previously explored, repentance is not sufficiently experienced through remorse or regret. True repentance is a change of attitude and understanding and overcomes the need for rationalization, reversal of the charge, or shifting the blame. Repentance is the interior desire to take the exterior action to repair the damage by being held accountable for one's complicity in the hurt and the promise not to repeat the offending behavior. The repentant personality permits the possibility of *metanoia*, a change of understanding, attitude, and heart. The self-absorption of narcissistic persons hinders their ability to repent and change their understanding of themselves and their actions. Research suggests that apologies for narcissistic people are more often a guise for self-justification; a defensive maneuver to deflect blame.[13] With limited capacity for empathy, little access to true humility, and a cache of self-protective reactions, engagement in repentance can appear impossible for those with these deficits in personality.

> *Genuine repentance eludes the self-preoccupied personality.*

Of course, in clinical cases narcissism is a legitimate personality disorder in need of treatment. In the context of this discussion—where God's grace interacts with genuine human desire for growth—the tendency toward and active engagement in such patterns of behavior are being explored as *solvable* constraints in recovering the inherent therapeutic power of the virtue of repentance. This discussion presumes that persons struggling with such tendencies can, with conscious attention to doing their emotional homework, and in freedom and grace, experience some success at overcoming the negative results of their nemesis, narcissism.

THE REPENTANT STEVEN AND THE FORGIVING JOSEPH

In the ideal yet realistic world of the forgiveness exchange, Bill and Marilyn and Marge and Susan would follow the path of Steven and Joseph. Highlighting the moments and movements in the Bernardin story with Steven Cook will illustrate the *kairos,* the *new time,* inaugurated by genuine repentance and the mutual desire for reconciliation. As figures 1 and 2 illustrate, reconciliation is the desired outcome of a successful forgiveness exchange. The Bernardin and Cook story forms the backdrop from which to explore the possibility of repentance in the other stories and the ways in which the Christian tradition can assist Marilyn and Bill and Susan and Marge in critically examining the possibilities for change of attitude, understanding, and heart in the midst of pain-filled time.

Joseph Bernardin, the one who experienced the offense, is the confronter in this story of transgression. The one experiencing the pain often initiates the confrontation and creates the condition to receive repentance from the offender. God works through the instrumentality of human beings just as grace builds on nature. As Joseph's heart turns in the direction of Steven, so too Steven's heart becomes ready to face the person whom he had so desperately wounded. Cardinal Bernardin often refers to the meeting that took place between himself and Steven as "grace-filled" with both desiring to bring closure to a painful rupture between them and within their own souls. A brief recap of that 1994 meeting based on published reports of the meeting suggests the dimensions of the pathway to repentance, forgiveness, and reconciliation.[14]

Immediately following Steven Cook's accusation against Joseph
Bernardin in November 1993, the cardinal wrote a letter requesting
that they meet. Steven never received this initial invitation. After
Steven's recantation of the charges, the cardinal made another effort
to connect with Steven, in Cardinal Bernardin's words, "to bring closure to the traumatic events of the last winter by personally letting
him know that I harbored no ill feelings toward him. Steven replied
that he wanted to meet with me to apologize for the embarrassment
and hurt he had caused. In other words, we both sought reconciliation."

> "*Steven's apology was simple, direct, deeply moving. I
> accepted his apology.*"

Bernardin's second invitation to meet and confront the issue
between them grew from the cardinal's processing of the pain of the
accusation and its implications for his own self-understanding.
Steven's positive reply to the invitation for a confrontation indicated
his disposition toward and readiness for repentance. The cardinal
empathically read the cue that Steven needed the opportunity to face
him person to person. After the meeting, Bernardin reported that
"Steven's apology was simple, direct, deeply moving. I accepted his
apology . . . I also told him that while I would not want to go through
such a humiliating experience again, nonetheless it had contributed to
my own spiritual growth and made me more compassionate."
Bernardin did not avoid direct confrontation with his accuser.
Steven made his amends directly and sincerely without recourse to
rationalization or minimization of the impact of his accusation on the
life of the cardinal. Since Steven had previously recanted and all
charges had been withdrawn, Bernardin had no apparent need to seek
an interpersonal encounter with Steven. Even though the cardinal had
clearly done his own intrapsychic spiritual and emotional homework,
he needed a face-to-face meeting. Reconciliation would flow from the
repentance offered and the forgiveness given and received in the context of this actual encounter of one man with his accuser. It is important to note that both Joseph and Steven had a friend present to
support each in and through a difficult moment. The presence of

these friends underscores the essentially relational and communal nature of Christian forgiveness. The celebration of the sacraments of Reconciliation and Eucharist by all present points to the natural flow from the pain-filled dimension of the encounter to the peace-filled ritualizing of forgiveness given and received.

"Before Steven left," Bernardin reported, "he told me that a big burden had been lifted from him. He felt healed and at peace. He also asked me to tell the story of his reconciliation. . . . I promised him I would and that I would walk with him in the weeks and months ahead." The cardinal ended his recollection of this meeting by saying: "Happily, our *exchange* [italics ours] and the celebration of the sacraments were the instruments God used to give him the peace and courage he needs in the time he has left." At the time of this encounter, Steven was dying from AIDS. Five months after this event, Bernardin himself was diagnosed with cancer. They talked on the telephone regularly and remained loyally attentive to each other to the end of their lives.

> *"He also asked me to tell the story of his reconciliation. . . .*
> *I promised him I would."*

This story of Joseph and Steven prompts the question whether such an exchange can take place only between the highly skilled, the exceptionally holy, or the dying? Is it actually possible for the ordinary person to make his or her way through the maze of interpersonal conflict that fractures the flow of love and trust in relationships of consequence? Some say that the energy investment and personal courage of the cardinal's and Steven Cook's story is more than what can be expected from most people. However, change of understanding and willingness to repent are the action of grace breaking into human desire for healing and restoration of love torn asunder. Humans must strive toward and do the hard and hopeful work of negotiating the scary and graced terrain of actually believing that they can overcome their narcissistic tendencies and repent. Through repentance, humans can be forgiven for intentionally or unintentionally inflicting wounds and can enter the experience of a reconciliation that lasts into eternity. Yes, more often than we may want to admit, it is possible to finish unfinished business in the thoughtful, courageous, discerning, and utterly human and graced manner that the story of Steven and Joseph reveals.

APPLICATION

Neither remorse nor regret nor rationalization is repentance. Repentance focuses on the offensive deed and its impact on the offended, but remorse and regret focus on the perpetrator and the repercussions he or she may encounter. Repentance is a change of understanding about the deed, but remorse and regret simply describe the uncomfortable feeling about the deed. Remorse and regret are feelings that may prompt those who harm us to a change of understanding, but these feelings alone are not repentance. Rationalization is an attempt to justify actions by an appeal to internal or external circumstances. It focuses on the offender and minimizes the offense. The perpetrator reasons that the way he or she is or the way the circumstances are explains and justifies the offensive action.

Repentance requires an interior mental and spiritual openness to be self-critical and nondefensive enough to accept the possibility of having caused harm to another. True repentance is a change of attitude and understanding and overcomes the need for rationalization, reversal of the charge, or shifting the blame. Repentance is the interior desire to take the exterior action to repair the damage by being held accountable for one's complicity in the hurt and the promise not to repeat the offending behavior. Ask yourself the following questions.

- Is my personality a repentance-sensitive or a repentance-challenged personality?

- How often have I felt regret or remorse and mistaken those feelings for authentic repentance?

- Am I prone to rationalizing my behavior when it produces unanticipated problems with others?

- Do my emotional and spiritual processes often begin with reversing the charge or shifting the blame so that I do not have to consider the possibility of my having caused harm to another?

Several human virtues characterize the repentance-sensitive personality. These virtues include (1) compassion in contrast to an unfeeling attitude, (2) empathy in contrast to narcissistic self-absorption, (3) humility in contrast to self-aggrandizement, (4) gratitude in contrast to resentment, and (5) largesse of mind and heart in contrast to self-protection and defensiveness.

Compassion means to feel with the suffering of another. It is an uncritical interior emotional movement in response to another's pain or suffering. Empathy is an active effort to critically understand another person's perceptions or experience as if you were that other person, rather than judging the other from the perspective of your own experience. Thus, compassion is passive; empathy is active.

While the distinction is subtle, engaging and nurturing both these characteristics in your personality can enrich your interior life and your relationship with others. Nurturing compassion and empathy are the only antidotes for combating unhealthy narcissism.

♦ Consider each virtue and how it manifests itself in your life. Are you aware of these virtues as healing arts at your disposal? How do you cultivate these virtues and your habitual ways of acting and relating? How do you experience compassion, empathy, humility, gratitude, and largesse as therapeutic both interiorly toward yourself and interpersonally?

♦ Are you aware of the presence and operation of the vices of lack of compassion, excessive self-preoccupation, inflation of your ego, tendencies toward resentments, and narrowness of thinking and acting?

Human beings must strive toward the hard and hopeful work of negotiating the scary and graced terrain of actually believing they can overcome their narcissistic tendencies and repent.

♦ Imaginatively enter a dialogue between your narcissistic self and your repentant self. Use your own story of fracture in relationship as a backdrop or context for the dialogue and give free reign to these dimensions of your personality to interact.

♦ What do you hear yourself saying? What insights emerge for you in dealing with your relational dilemma? What did you learn from the interplay of these selves within yourself?

Place yourself on the continuum of virtue to vice,
and reflect upon your honest self-appraisal.

compassion   unfeeling attitude
//
1   2   3   4   5   6   7   8   9   10

empathy   narcissistic self-absorption
//
1   2   3   4   5   6   7   8   9   10

humility   self-aggrandizement
//
1   2   3   4   5   6   7   8   9   10

gratitude   resentment
//
1   2   3   4   5   6   7   8   9   10

largesse of mind and heart   self-protection/defensiveness
//
1   2   3   4   5   6   7   8   9   10

NOTES

1. Robert A. Emmons, "Personality and Forgiveness," in *Forgiveness: Theory, Research, and Practice,* ed. Michael E. McCullough, Kenneth I. Pargament, and Carl E. Thoresen (New York: Guilford Press, 2000), 171.

2. Heinrich Schipperges, *Hildegard of Bingen: Healing and the Nature of the Cosmos* (Princeton: Markus Wiener Publishers, 1997), 87-110.

3. Wanda M. Malcolm and Leslie S. Greenberg, "Forgiveness as Process of Change in Individual Psychotherapy," in *Forgiveness: Theory, Research, and Practice,* ed. Michael E. McCullough, Kenneth I. Pargament, and Carl E. Thoresen (New York: Guilford Press, 2000), 180.

4. Emmons, "Personality," 164.

5. For a detailed analysis of the relationship between human development and the stages of adult maturation in faith, see James W. Fowler, *Becoming Adult, Becoming Christian* (San Francisco: Harper & Row, 1984).

6. Robert A. Emmons, "Is Spirituality an Intelligence? Motivation, Cognition, and the Psychology of Ultimate Concerns," *International Journal for the Psychology of Religion,* forthcoming.

7. L. Sperry and H. L. Ansbacher, "The Concept of Narcissism and Narcissistic Personality Disorder," in *Psychopathology and Psychotherapy*, ed. L. Sperry and J. Carlson (Washington, D.C.: Accelerated Development, 1996), 349.

8. Emmons, "Personality," 164.

9. R. Raskin and H. Terry, "A Principal Components Analysis of the Narcissistic Personality Inventory and Further Evidence of Its Construct Validity," *Journal of Personality and Social Psychology* 54 (1988): 896.

10. Emmons, "Personality," 161–63.

11. Ibid., 161–64.

12. Jeffrey Brandsma, "Forgiveness: A Dynamic, Theological and Therapeutic Analysis," *Pastoral Psychology* 31 (fall 1982): 41.

13. Emmons, "Personality," 167.

14. For Cardinal Bernardin's own rendering of the story, see Joseph Cardinal Bernardin, *The Gift of Peace* (Chicago: Loyola University Press, 1997), 15–41.

CHAPTER 8

Biblical Insights into the Transferal of Responsibility and Release

⌒

I N CONTRAST TO THE ADAGE to forgive and forget—implicit in the intrapsychic model of forgiveness—the Bible advocates a response toward offenders that begins with confrontation and accountability. Also in contrast to the adage and the intrapsychic model, the Bible links forgiveness with repentance. If a transgressor repents, then the offended is responsible to forgive the offender and the relationship between the two is restored. What about those instances, however, when those who wrong us display an unrepentant attitude toward us? When offenders remain obstinate even after confrontation, what response does the Bible recommend? Jesus provides the answer to this question and demonstrates the model response.

TRANSFERAL OF RESPONSIBILITY

The numerous scripture passages cited in the previous chapters show that Jesus repeatedly confronted his generation with the need to repent of wrongdoing. Throughout his public life, he confronted the same people again and again in an effort to hold them accountable. When his generation finally crucified him and no one rose to his defense, his imminent death prohibited him from holding his contemporaries accountable any longer. Just before he died, Jesus uttered those familiar words from the cross, "Father, forgive them, they know not what they do" (Luke 23:34 *NAB*). These words express the recommended biblical response toward recalcitrant offenders.

> *"Father, forgive them, they know not what they do." (Luke 23:34 NAB)*

At first glance, these words appear to sanction the intrapsychic model and the adage to forgive and forget even when our offenders remain unrepentant. After all, Jesus prayed for the forgiveness of his tormentors even while they were crucifying him. Jesus' prayer certainly reveals his willingness to forgive. Nevertheless, a crucial distinction exists between Jesus' prayer for his Father to forgive his persecutors and Jesus' own utterance of forgiveness. Jesus does not say to his persecutors, "I forgive you." Instead, he prays for God to forgive them. His prayer transfers the process of forgiveness to God. God now becomes responsible for holding these culprits accountable and for forgiving them should they repent.

Since God's forgiveness is always linked to repentance, Jesus' prayer does not effect the immediate forgiveness of these offenders. Indeed, Peter speaks through the Holy Spirit at Pentecost and accuses these crowds of crucifying Jesus (Acts 2:24). Peter's call for them to repent and receive forgiveness is superfluous if Jesus' prayer already effected their forgiveness (Acts 2:38). Jesus' words from the cross do not sanction the adage to forgive an unrepentant offender. Instead, these words recommend transferring the responsibility of forgiving a recalcitrant offender to God.

Similar words spoken by Stephen also reiterate this recommendation. Stephen's confrontational speech, which exposes the failures of his fellow Jews, elicits their fury. Prior to his dying beneath a barrage of stones, Stephen prays, "Lord, do not hold this sin against them" (Acts 7:60). Following Jesus' example, he does not say, "I forgive you." Instead, he transfers the responsibility of accountability and forgiveness to the Lord. His prayer is similar to Jesus' prayer on the cross and does not effect the forgiveness of his murderers, as the example of Saul/Paul demonstrates.

> *"Lord, do not hold this sin against them." (Acts 7:60)*

Saul/Paul participates with this crowd in Stephen's murder. Sometime later, Saul/Paul is accosted on the Damascus road by the Lord, who does not proclaim his forgiveness but asks, "Saul, Saul, why are you persecuting me?" (Acts 9:4). Saul/Paul's forgiveness is inextricably linked to his repentant attitude demonstrated by his three-day fast (Acts 9:9). Were he to have remained recalcitrant, it is unlikely that Saul/Paul would have survived his Damascus road experience, and he never would have become the great apostle of Christendom. The example of Saul/Paul demonstrates that Stephen's dying prayer does not effect the forgiveness of his persecutors but transfers the responsibility for confronting and forgiving to the Lord when Stephen is no longer able to hold his tormentors accountable.

Both Jesus' and Stephen's dying prayer model the recommended biblical response toward unrepentant offenders. When we are no longer able to hold our offender accountable, we transfer the responsibility of forgiveness to God. God then assumes the obligation to hold our offender accountable and to pressure him or her toward repentance so that genuine forgiveness can ensue. Neither Jesus' nor Stephen's prayer models forgiving an intractable offender who refuses to repent. Neither prayer sanctions the surface, cheap forgiveness that often results from following the adage to forgive and forget. Furthermore, neither prayer is an instance of intrapsychic forgiveness. Both prayers recognize the intricate connection between repentance and forgiveness for genuine forgiveness to occur between offender and offended.

BIBLICAL TRANSFERAL,
NOT PSYCHOLOGICAL TRANSFERENCE

This notion of transferal in the Bible is not *transference*, a term used in clinical psychology to describe a client's transfer of past emotional attachments in an earlier developmental relationship onto the therapist.[1] In transference, a client transfers to the therapist prior positive or negative attitudes and feelings toward a parent or other significant person from a past developmental stage. Neither the prayer of Jesus nor that of Stephen is an example of transference. Jesus and Stephen do not treat God as a therapist by transferring their feelings and attitudes toward the crowd to God. Instead, they transfer the responsibility of the crowd's accountability and forgiveness to God. This transfer releases both Jesus and Stephen from expending further mental, emotional, and physical energy in their relationship with the crowd. God is now the confronter and the one who works to effect the crowd's repentance and forgiveness. Even though it affects emotions, the biblical transferal of responsibility is thus very different from the psychological transference of emotions and attitudes.

> *The transferal of responsibility recommended in the Bible is not psychological transference.*

Clearly, the transferal of responsibility recommended in the Bible is not psychological transference. In transferal of responsibility, our negative and immature or arrested attitudes and feelings are not foisted upon either God or our offender. Rather, our transferal of responsibility is a mature, conscious, and rational response to a relational impasse. When our offender refuses to repent, we cannot forgive without condoning an unjust situation and enabling an unjust person to continue destructive behavior. When we have responsibly confronted our offender and are no longer able to hold our offender accountable, we should make a mature, conscious decision to transfer our offender to God. In contrast to psychological transference, this transferal of responsibility is both rational and relationally healthy. It changes our relationship with our offender and protects us from the negative and painful effects of continued engagement with a recalcitrant offender.

BIBLICAL TRANSFERAL, INTERPERSONAL AND NOT INTRAPSYCHIC

This transferal of responsibility in the New Testament is also not simply an intrapsychic experience. More than a mental activity, the prayers of Jesus and Stephen affirm that a divine dimension exists in every human relationship. A relationship between two people is actually a relationship of the two people with God. Jesus said, "Where two or three are gathered together in my name, there am I in the midst of them" (Matt. 18:20; cf. 1 Cor. 5:4). Transferal of responsibility recognizes this triadic nature of every human relationship and provides release for us when we encounter a recalcitrant offender. After the offended fulfills the responsibility of confronting and of holding the offender accountable and the offender remains unrepentant, the offended may give this responsibility to God, who is the third person in the relationship. The offended is released from further victimization by the recalcitrant offender, who is now confronted directly by God. This transferal of responsibility is thus an interpersonal rather than an intrapsychic experience.

> *This transferal of responsibility in the New Testament is not simply an intrapsychic experience.*

BIBLICAL TRANSFERAL—A CHANGED RELATIONSHIP

When we transfer the responsibility for our offender to God, we do not abandon the relationship. Transferal does not "flush" the offender from our lives. By transferring the responsibility to God, we remain in relationship with our offender, but the relationship changes. We permit God to assume the responsibility for our offender and for making the unjust situation right. We are free from obligation to our offender even while remaining in relationship with her or him and with God.

The story of Samuel and King Saul illustrates the change in a relationship that transferal of responsibility effects. Twice Samuel confronts Saul for disobeying God, and Saul refuses to repent on both occasions (1 Sam. 13, 15). Continued confrontation is dangerous for Samuel (1 Sam. 16:2), and so he never sees Saul again (1 Sam. 15:35). Nevertheless, Samuel grieves over Saul and the fractured relationship to the point that Samuel's life comes to a standstill. God then speaks to Samuel, "How long will you grieve for Saul, whom I have rejected as king of Israel?" (1 Sam. 16:1). God now assumes the responsibility for Saul, and Samuel is free to proceed with his life. God instructs Samuel, "Fill your horn with oil, and be on your way. I am sending you to Jesse of Bethlehem, for I have chosen my king from among his sons" (1 Sam. 16:1). Samuel then performs the most significant achievement of his life by anointing David to be king.

> *God assumes responsibility for our offender. We are freed from our obligation toward the offender.*

Samuel's transferal of Saul to God not only frees Samuel but also forces Saul to deal directly with God. Under increasing pressure from God, Saul eventually seeks to reestablish his former relationship with Samuel by conjuring him from the dead to tell Saul what he should do (1 Sam. 28:15–19). Whereas Samuel's confronting Saul on two prior occasions is ineffective, God's confrontation (1 Sam. 28:15) now brings Saul to the place where he is willing to listen to Samuel, who once again confronts Saul (1 Sam. 28:18–19). Samuel reminds Saul that his disobedient and unrepentant lifestyle results in his demise and that he would be with Samuel in less than a day (1 Sam. 28:17–19). God makes this final confrontation possible and places Samuel in a position where Saul cannot harm him. Whereas transferal frees Samuel to perform the greatest achievement of his life, it forces an unrepentant Saul to deal directly with God and to contend with increasing pressure to repent.

> *Transferal is not an abandonment of the relationship.*

The story of Samuel and Saul illustrates that our transferring the responsibility for a recalcitrant offender to God is not an abandonment of the relationship. Transferal recognizes that we have fulfilled our responsibility for holding our offender accountable, and this responsibility now falls to God. Recalcitrant offenders usually resist human efforts at confrontation, but God's confrontation assumes such divine intensity that unrepentant offenders are often brought to their senses. As in the case of Saul, God's confrontation frequently forces an offender to attempt reestablishing the relationship with the offended. Being sensitive to this moment, we should take advantage of the situation brought about by God's confrontation and consummate a successful forgiveness exchange. If we have simply "flushed" the offender from our life, we may miss this divine opportunity to heal a fractured relationship. Thus, transferal does not permit us to abandon the relationship with our offender but to entrust this relationship to

God and wait for God to effect the needed resolution. The story of Samuel and Saul demonstrates that this resolution may occur even after death.

APPROPRIATE SITUATIONS FOR TRANSFERAL

The transferal of responsibility recommended by the prayers of both Jesus and Stephen is particularly appropriate when an offender has died. Death prohibits us from confronting a deceased offender and receiving the repentance necessary for extending an offer of forgiveness. In this situation, we often feel stuck with no way to resolve our anger, resentment, or bitterness toward the one who harmed us. Children of abusive, deceased parents are particularly vulnerable to this trap. Carrying their painful emotions into adulthood, many seek release from their destructive memories. Intrapsychic attempts at forgiveness without repentance can force the abused victim to expend enormous amounts of psychic energy to "normalize" a situation that was and remains abnormal. Transferal of the abusive parents to God, however, enables such victims to "get on" with their lives while continuing to recognize the injustice inflicted on them by someone who was supposed to be their protector. The victim no longer takes responsibility for the perpetrator or for what happened. God takes and holds this responsibility. In faith, the victim transfers the abusive, deceased parent to God and trusts God to resolve this fractured, painful relationship in God's time.

> *Transferal of responsibility is particularly appropriate when an offender has died.*

Of course, transferal is also appropriate in situations when our unrepentant offender is still living. In all situations when confrontation and accountability are no longer possible or advisable, we may find release from an arrogant offender by transferring the offender to God. Confrontation is sometimes impossible because of the internal emotions of the offended. When our anger toward an unrepentant offender turns to bitterness, it is probably time for us to transfer the responsibility for this offender to God. At other times, confrontation may be impossible because of the offender. When the offender is dangerous, we should not confront directly. An abused partner should not personally confront the abuser. As long as there are social and legal means to hold the offender accountable, transferal is probably premature. When all reasonable means of confrontation and accountability are exhausted, however, transferal is appropriate and serves the well-being of both the offended and ultimately the offender.

The prayers of both Jesus and Stephen as well as the story of Samuel and Saul recommend a response to fractured relationships that is far more healthy than either the adage to forgive and forget or intrapsychic approaches to forgiveness that limit the process to internal feelings and thoughts. When the ideal of confrontation, repentance, and forgiveness cannot be achieved, the Bible recommends interpersonal transferal as the appropriate response. Transferring an obstinate offender to God allows us to continue recognizing the injustice of the situation and still find psychological and spiritual release. Transferal places such an offender in the hands of God, who is best able to deal with obstinacy and arrogance.

> *When our anger toward an unrepentant offender turns to bitterness, it is time to transfer the responsibility for this offender to God.*

The Bible insightfully recognizes the importance of this response toward an unrepentant offender for preserving our well-being. Continued contact between us and an arrogant offender often results in feelings of resentment, bitterness, and hatred. When we have exhausted every means of holding our offender accountable, we should transfer responsibility for this recalcitrant person to God. This transferal provides emotional, psychological, and spiritual freedom for us even while the unresolved relationship with our offender remains. This transferal does not require us to commit an unjust act by exonerating an arrogant transgressor. By transferring the responsibility of confrontation and forgiveness to God, we are able to recognize the continued injustice of the situation without being chained to our offender. By this transferring of responsibility, the Bible provides for our well-being in the face of an arrogant offender.

APPLICATION

♦ Jesus' and Stephen's prayer recommends transferal of responsibility when faced with obstinate offenders. Name an offender who is so obstinate that despite your best effort he or she refused to take responsibility for harmful actions.

♦ How did you handle such an offender? Did you try exoneration or intrapsychic forgiveness? How did these strategies affect you and your offender?

♦ Have you ever invited God into this broken relationship by transferring the responsibility of forgiving this offender to God? If you have, how did you feel afterwards toward this offender, yourself, and God? If you have not, do you think this might be the right time to make such a transferal?

♦ What do you think will happen if you try to transfer someone to God before you have fulfilled your role in the accountability process?

♦ Reflect on those persons who have wounded you deeply but refused to repent and with whom you have never found resolution. For each person, ask yourself if you still have some obligation in the confrontation and accountability process. If so, you may want to reread chapters 4 and 5.

♦ If you feel you have done everything you can do and the time is right, why not begin to transfer such persons to God right now by praying the following prayer?

> ♦ "Loving God, I give _____ to you now. You know how _____ has hurt me but refused to own responsibility. I am at the end of my efforts to hold _____ accountable and so I transfer _____ to you. I recognize that the relationship between _____ and me remains unresolved, but I can no longer carry _____. I entrust _____ to you and believe that in your infinite mystery you will continue to confront and hold _____ accountable. I give _____ into your hands and ask you to help me to be freed from the pain and

to trust that your mercy is big enough to care for both of us. Amen."

NOTES

1. David G. Benner and Peter C. Hill, eds., *Baker Encyclopedia of Psychology and Counseling* (Grand Rapids: Baker, 1999), 1224; Benjamin B. Wolman, ed., *Dictionary of Behavioral Science* (New York: Van Nostrand Reinhold Company, 1973), 390.

CHAPTER 9

The Grace and Burden
of Unfinished Business

∽

T HE CHRISTIAN FORGIVENESS exchange supports the well-being of the offended in the face of an arrogant and unrepentant offender. There are those situations in which the one offended cannot forgive an unrepentant offender. In these situations, the only and best recourse is to transfer the responsibility of confrontation and forgiveness to God. God's largesse, which defies human imagination, can "hold" the unrepentant offender accountable through the mysterious "cord of compassion" (Hos. 11:4 RSV), God's continuous unbroken love for all those fashioned in God's own image. It is in these situations that eschatological theology—the study of the ultimate destiny of humankind and the world—provides a theological and spiritual solution to serious unfinished business.

PURGATORY REVISITED: A SPECIAL KIND OF HOPE

The word *purgatory* may seem strange in a contemporary text such as this, and this word may appear anachronistic to many twenty-first century Catholics and Protestants. Yet this Catholic Christian teaching provides a way to deal with unrepentant and unhealed fractures of love and trust that splinter relationships even to the point of death. A renewed consideration of purgatory may provide needed resolutions to some terribly painful unfinished human situations. This section will focus briefly on the older notion of purgatory and move into the contemporary teaching as a possible psychotheological remedy to unfinished business.

The word *purgatory* does not occur in the Bible, but the idea arises in the extreme situation recounted by 1–2 Maccabees. These books narrate the life-and-death struggles of the Jews against the Seleucid rulers, who attempt to force the Jews to become Greeks. The Seleucids attack the Jews on the Sabbath day because they know the Jewish Law prohibits fighting on that day. At first, the Jews refuse to fight and exhort one another, "Let us die without reproach" (1 Macc. 2:37). Realizing they will all perish unless they fight on the Sabbath, the Jews later decide, "Let us fight against anyone who attacks us on the Sabbath" (1 Macc. 2:41). This decision raises the question of what will happen to a soldier who dies fighting on the Sabbath. At the judgment, will God condemn him as a transgressor of the Law, or will God make other provisions? The Jews adopt the latter alternative and develop a theological position that forms the basis for the Roman Catholic doctrine of purgatory.

This theological position is more explicit in 2 Macc. 12:38–46. This passage narrates an incident in which Jewish soldiers die transgressing the Law. The issue here is not violating the Sabbath but wearing amulets to pagan deities. The Jewish survivors of the battle pray "that the sinful deed might be fully blotted out" (2 Macc. 12:42), and they take up a collection to send "to Jerusalem to provide for an expiatory sacrifice" (2 Macc. 12:43). The survivors thus "make atonement for the dead that they might be freed from this sin" (2 Macc. 12:46). This passage clearly articulates that those who die with unresolved sin can be purged by the activities of the living, especially by prayers and sacrifices. The theological position adopted by the Jews in this extreme situation contains the basic elements of the later and more fully developed doctrine of purgatory.

Interestingly, the fathers of the church, not unlike ourselves, struggled with how to understand the "things" associated with the end-time, such as God's final judgment, heaven, hell, and the second coming of Christ. While Augustine spoke of an "intermediate realm" after death, the doctrine of purgatory was not really articulated until the twelfth century. Not surprisingly, purgatory was an issue in the Reformation and the subsequent Council of Trent (1545–1563). This council mightily reaffirmed the retributive nature of purgatory, and much of the Catholic theology on purgatory is derived from the workings of this council.

For hundreds of years following the Council of Trent, purgatory was a "given" for most Catholics, as one assumed that one almost never "got into heaven" without "doing time" in purgatory. As already noted in the brief discussion on the evolution of the sacrament of Penance in chapter 3 above, the Catholic Church held a very legalistic position on sin and entry into eternal salvation. Indulgences, saying prayers, or doing acts of charity that brought a reduction of time in purgatory became the vehicles to free a loved one from the punishment of purgatory and win the peace of God's eternity. Purgatory was a grim reality that faced believers at the end of life, and Masses said and intercessory prayers offered for the dead were their best hope of a speedy entry into God's eternal kingdom. In this theological vision, the suffering endured in purgatory was inflicted from outside the soul and cast in imagery of fire and pain. Purgatory was not quite hell, but a close second.

Surprising for some, the Catholic Church never abandoned its theology of purgatory, even though this doctrine has had little emphasis since the Second Vatican Council. Quite simply, the current Catholic position on purgatory teaches that individuals carry with them into eternity the responsibility for unrepented sin. As has been the case throughout Christian history and with the current Catholic magisterium, there is no information on the detailed structure of the process of purgatory, especially its connection to a temporal understanding of time and place. The reality of purgatory, like so many other realities of faith, falls into the realm of mystery.

Current Catholic theology on the subject holds, "Purgatory is best understood as *a process by which we are purged of our residual selfishness so that we can really become one with God who is totally oriented to other, i.e., a self-giving God.*"[1] In contemporary doctrine, the suffering associated with purgatory is not inflicted from the outside, but *"the intrinsic pain that we feel when we are asked to surrender our ego-centered self so that the God-centered loving self may take its place."*[2] In psychological terms, the purgative experience, whether on the earthly side of this life or in the eternal dimension of the next life, holds the solution to the tight grip of narcissism that mires us in an unyielding selfishness and ego-centeredness that stifle the emergence of the therapeutic virtues of empathy, humility, gratitude, and largesse of mind and heart.

> *"Purgatory is best understood as a process by which we are purged of our residual selfishness so that we can really become one with God."*

Because human beings carry into their final days the power and possibility of free will, the Catholic Church believes that such a "state" exists even though it cannot be thoroughly defined or described. In addition, the grace of God is a gift not only for this time (*chronos* and conscious *kairos*) but also for eternity, beyond all human understanding of time. A theology of the human person takes the position that just as all humans are created in *imago dei*, so also all have an innate or inherent drive for union and reunion with the Creator. God's compassionate desire is to receive each home to her or his final destiny, where each will reside forever in the fullness of the loving embrace of God. While rife with disorienting and painful obstacles, the striving for resolution can indeed be accomplished in the gift of our biological life span. Such striving in faith throughout our journey in life is understood as both graced and joyful—and marked, at times, by a kind of purgatory-on-earth. Therefore, the church makes an assumption that in death most people fold gently and immediately into God's embrace. The beatific vision—the immediate consciousness of God face-to-face—is the eschatological destiny of all humanity and, indeed, the immediate experience of most at the time of death.

> *When one cannot forgive an unrepentant offender, the only and best recourse is to transfer the responsibility of confrontation and forgiveness to God.*

The Christian faith must, however, allow for some graced process beyond limited human mental constructs to account for those who choose to die unrepentantly refusing to face the reality of their egocentricity, unattended narcissism, or hardness of heart. What is the ultimate destiny of those who die in unrepentant silence, apparently obstinate to the end? What is theologically available to an unrepentant perpetrator when the one offended finally in trust transfers responsibility to God? What happens if the unrepentant person dies unrepentant to the end? It is possible for a person to die having failed to face the unfinished business of her or his sinful patterns, having ignored the offer of grace to transcend egocentric preoccupation, and having refused to strive to heal the reality of fractured relationships and love torn asunder? Purgatory provides for *a special kind of hope* for such persons in the process of growth and maturation that follows death. This hope enables such persons to face the reality of defects that remain an obstacle to their full communion with God. Catholic theology teaches, "Only to the extent that this growth in love is painful can we speak of suffering in purgatory."[3] God has more options than temporal reference alone. For human beings, what we consciously experience is the only time available to live life, grow, make relationships, and set things right that have gone asunder. In God, chronological time is no longer operational; eternal time opens up options that exist beyond human imagination or comprehension.

ON LIFE AFTER DEATH

This text has already credited Elisabeth Kübler-Ross, psychiatrist and pioneer in the field of death and dying, with developing the emotional and spiritual issue known as unfinished business. In the last decade, most of Dr. Kübler-Ross's work has focused on the experience of the afterlife that she believes exists because of her extensive research with the dying and those who have experienced near-death experiences. She has gone so far as to suggest that the way people finish their unfinished business "on the other side" is through a process she calls the "life review." She writes:

> During this review of your earthly life you will not blame God for your fate, but you will know that you yourself were your own worst enemy since you are now accusing yourself of having neglected so many opportunities to grow. Now you know that long ago when your house burnt down, when your child died, when your husband hurt himself, or when you yourself suffered a heart attack, all fatal blows were merely some of the many possibilities for you to grow: to grow in understanding, to grow in love, to grow in all things which we still have to learn. . . . You start to look at life differently. . . . [You] become aware of [your] potential, of what [you] could be like, of what [you] have been like. . . . [You] review and evaluate [your] total existence . . . without negative emotions, [you] embrace [yourself] as [you] truly are and merge completely into the Source of Light.[4]

From Kübler-Ross's perspective, entry into eternity is a process, and human mental constructs of time fail to adequately interpret the time it takes an individual soul to process into eternity. Kübler-Ross is convinced that the light of death and the awareness of being in the presence of an all-embracing Love enable one to look back on one's entire life from the first day until the last.

This recapitulation happens in a state of consciousness unable to be explained in humanly limited terms. The state of being, however, permits a survey of the memory of the whole of one's life and all the consequences resulting from one's thoughts, words, and deeds. Kübler-Ross suggests that this life review can take place precisely because the soul has been transformed in such a way as to be able to receive the reality of God's pervasive unconditional love and grace, and thereby face the fullness of truth. This life review takes place in an atmosphere devoid of any condemnation.

Her work on this "intermediate state" in the afterlife is remarkably consistent with Catholic theology. Theologian Karl Rahner has said that purgatory is best understood as a state beyond the grasp of complete intelligibility and the strictures of space and time. Rahner speculated that what goes on in purgatory is a process by which what has been repressed or hidden from a soul is manifested within the human heart. The substance of the self-reflection has already been present in the depth of that person's being, and yet he or she has resisted the review of deeds, repressed the activity of the conscience, and allowed a masquerade (*persona*) of one's true nature that has been lost to the person through the misdirection of the exercise of his or her freedom. Thus, this process of integration whereby after death the totality of the human person is enlisted against the resistance arising from one's own sin issues *without fail* in communion with the beatific vision.[5]

> *Whatever hell is, it is about the conscious, total rejection of the embrace of truth offered in love and the subsequent eternal void.*

Tragically, human freedom, even in the post-death realm, permits one to ultimately reject the offer of God's redeeming love. Richard McBrien says, "*Although the church has always taught that we have the capacity to reject God fundamentally (mortal sin), it has never taught that there are, in fact, persons in hell."*[6] He further says that it is beyond human grasp to ascertain if anyone, including ourselves, has finally, definitively, and nonreversibly rejected God *"even in an act which appears on the surface to be of such a kind."*[7] Whatever hell is, it is about the conscious, total rejection of the embrace of truth offered in love and the subsequent eternal void. Hell, derived from the Greek word meaning "the realm of the dead" is not an outcome of divine vindictiveness; rather hell is "God's yielding to human freedom."[8] Hell is absolute and irrevocable isolation. The horror of this mystery defies words. Because of freedom, hell must remain within the repertoire of human choice, yet the power of God's mercy and love "can do immeasurably more than we can ask or imagine" (Eph. 3:20).

Because of freedom and grace, even after death, God works with all irresolution, unfinished intrapsychic and interpersonal business, which remains unhealed in the process of moving from the earthly to the eternal realm. Taken together, the insights of Kübler-Ross and contemporary Catholic doctrine suggest a pastoral theology of purgatory that provides the occasion for post-death repentance and change of attitude and understanding.

LIVING UNTIL WE DIE

People who choose in life to accept the burden of their own personalities and carry the cross that bears their own name are those willing to learn the art form of doing their emotional and spiritual homework. Those persons are afraid neither of living nor of dying.

In the case of eighty-year-old Marge and her daughter, the future looks bleak for Marge's repentance, a softening and the turning of attitudes, understanding, and hearts in the direction of healing the fracture of love and trust. For such to take place, Marge must forgo her sense of being the offended offender and reach out, now over the span of more than four years, and reconnect with her daughter. Who could help Marge consider the call to repentance? Might the Minister of Communion who makes weekly Sunday visits to Marge be confidentially apprised by Marge's other children of the stalemate between Marge and her daughter Susan? More than likely the pastoral care home visitor has already heard parts of the sad story. In the spiritual context of the weekly visits, the lay minister could initiate conversation introducing the theme of the importance of completing unfinished business during the final years of life.

Another venue for repentance might arise from Susan. Realizing that time is limited to heal this rift, Susan may choose to forgo the requirement of initiation by her mother and ask for a meeting to see if healing is possible. Since Marge has previously indicated that she expects an apology from her daughter and son-in-law, Susan may announce to her mother that she harbors no ill feeling toward her and wishes to return to the hurtful moment for the purpose of retrieving a more authentic relationship. For the forgiveness exchange to be successful, the persons involved must be willing to reexperience the hurt within a new context. Susan's intent would be to prompt a sincere dialogue with her mother by placing the past hurt of years ago in the less threatening and more empathic context of the present. It is important to note that while Marge's age and history of depression pose particular challenges, Susan is not in a situation that suggests she exonerate her mother. Age is not a barrier to the action of God's moving Marge to repent and engage in the forgiveness exchange.

> *For the forgiveness exchange to be successful, the persons involved must be willing to reexperience the hurt within a new context.*

To illustrate this point, Rahner, not long before his death at eighty, was asked what a theologian had to say about the significance of living a long life. He replied that old age was a grace, a special task, and a danger. He said, "As long as these people [the elderly] possess their inner personal freedom, they are still able to turn meaningfully to God, to accept their life, which grows, of course, more and more restricted, with Christian patience, in hope of eternity. And, as a theologian, I can only say that for those, who out of pride or as a protest against life do not accept this, I have no other consolation."[9]

Marge's death, or her daughter's for that matter, will not end the unresolved conflicts. These issues do not evaporate with death; they submerge only to reemerge without permission into the lives of their loved ones, generation unto generation. Completing unfinished business is the best gift one can give to others and leave as a legacy in death. With so much hope within the operating theology of Christianity, there is also the tough conviction that there remain consequences—personal, interpersonal, familial, communal, and eternal—for those who refuse to do the work of their unfinished business.

Catholic theology has long held the position that in death we do not become blessed and graced by God in a way that is totally different from the way we have chosen to live the journey of our lives. Rahner has written that in death we do not become in God the totally unexpected; rather "the harvest of our earthly life will be inserted into God's life, our eternal life."[10] As has already been explored in this text, personal redemption is a process; salvation is progressive, interpersonal, and social. The striving for full human potential within the context of a loving life has to do with free will and God's grace working in tandem with our cooperation for us to embrace the often challenging reality that we will never be exempt from the gift and burden of living, living relationally, and living until we die.

APPLICATION

+ Prior to reading this chapter how would you have answered the question, What is the destiny of those who die unrepentant? Having read the chapter, is your answer now the same or different?

+ What most surprised you in reading this chapter?

+ What most disturbed you in reading this chapter?

+ What consoled you in reading this chapter?

+ Have you faced a situation where someone you loved died with significant unfinished business? In free-flow, uncensored writing, tell the story of this relationship and why you hold the conviction that the person died with unresolved relational business.

+ How have you attempted to draw closure on the relationship and find inner peace when the wounds remained untouched and unhealed due to the physical death of the beloved or once beloved offender?

♦ In what ways do the theology of this chapter and the practices described in this book provide insight into God's largesse and God's ability to work with an unrepentant offender even after death?

♦ Are you ready and willing to transfer the responsibility to God and open yourself to the experience of relief and release?

♦ Can you allow for a *special kind of hope* to resolve the unfinished business in the dimension of faith beyond the grasp of human comprehension?

NOTES

1. Richard McBrien, *Catholicism* (San Francisco: HarperCollins, 1994), 1168–69.

2. Ibid.

3. Wolfgang Beinert and Francis Schüssler-Fiorenza, eds., *Handbook of Catholic Theology* (New York: Crossroad, 1995), 563.

4. See Elisabeth Kübler-Ross, *On Life After Death* (Berkeley, Calif.: Celestial Arts Publishing, 1991).

5. Karl Lehmann and Albert Raffelt, eds., *Karl Rahner: The Content of Faith* (New York: Crossroad, 1994), 631–34.

6. McBrien, *Catholicism*, 957.

7. Ibid.

8. Ibid.

9. Paul Imhoff and Hubert Baillowons, eds., *Karl Rahner in Dialogue: Conversations and Interviews, 1965–1982* (New York: Crossroad, 1986), 242–43.

10. *Karl Rahner: I Remember*, trans. Harvey Egan (New York: Crossroad, 1985), 102.

CHAPTER 10

Concluding the Stories

∾

THE SABOTAGED FORGIVENESS EXCHANGE:
AN UNEXPECTED HEALING

THE SABOTAGED FORGIVENESS EXCHANGE between Marilyn and Bill has left Marilyn thinking she is doomed to hell. His unrepentant attitude and actions make it impossible for her to forgive him. She has confronted him, but he remains obstinate and arrogant. Other family members have also attempted to hold him accountable, but he refuses to own the offense and to offer sorrow at the hurt he has caused. Despite her best efforts, Marilyn cannot forgive Bill, and she feels doomed to alienation from God into eternity. What can Marilyn do? What should she do?

Marilyn's pastoral counselor encourages her to recognize that she has completed all the steps for which she is responsible. She has confronted Bill and involved other family members who have also attempted to hold him accountable. Continuing to hold Bill responsible would only result in her further victimization and in her deepening anger, bitterness, and depression. Her pastoral counselor advises her that it is time for her to transfer the responsibility for Bill's forgiveness to God.

Marilyn's journey to this point of transferal has been long and difficult, but now, instructed by her pastoral counselor, Marilyn prays:

Lord, I am ashamed of what has happened to me, and I am so angry at Bill for what he has done to me. You know I have tried to forgive him time and time again, Lord, but to forgive him would affirm that what

112

he did is resolved, and it is not. Lord, I have carried him far too long. The anger and bitterness are eating away at me. I cannot carry him any longer, and I give him to you right now. He now belongs to you. Please confront him and bring him to repentance. Thank you, Lord, for taking him and freeing me from this burden that has wrecked my life. Thank you. Thank you. Amen.

When Marilyn raises her head from prayer, she looks at her pastoral counselor and exclaims, "I am free! I am free! I am free! At long last, I am free!"

> *Continuing to hold Bill responsible would only result in her further victimization.*

Indeed, Marilyn's transferring Bill to God frees Marilyn. She no longer feels the need to focus on Bill and the rape that almost destroyed her life. When she sees Bill, she reminds God that Bill is now God's responsibility and not hers. She is released from her former focus on the pain and freed to engage in positive pursuits. While the scars left from the deep wounds of Bill's violently irresponsible action will always be with Marilyn, she is liberated from him and the responsibility to normalize her relationship with him. God now assumes this responsibility. Whereas Marilyn is free, Bill, as long as he remains obstinate, is bound to God's confrontation.

Throughout the years, Bill successfully resists all of Marilyn's and her family's efforts at confrontation. However, Bill now finds himself in the hands of a God whose ability to confront is mysteriously powerful. A few months after Marilyn transfers Bill to God, Bill accepts a job out-of-state and moves. Marilyn is elated. She no longer has to encounter him on a weekly basis. Shortly after Bill arrives at his new residence, his job is terminated, and he lacks the resources to return to his former home. God is at work breaking down Bill's arrogance and his obstinacy. God's confrontation will not cease into eternity until Bill accepts the responsibility for his unjust action and repents.

A few years pass, and Marilyn's grandmother dies. Marilyn's pastoral counselor is invited to officiate at the funeral. As the family enters, he notices that the funeral director seats Marilyn and Bill on opposite sides of the family section and thanks God for their separation from each other. After the ceremony, the pastoral counselor takes his place at the head of the casket and greets those who come to pay their last respects. Looking up, he sees Bill with Marilyn right behind him. Anxious about what may happen, he laments that such an insensitive funeral director is in charge.

He watches with apprehension as Bill quietly pays his last respects and turns to leave. Suddenly, Marilyn reaches out to Bill and with both hands grabs the lapels of his jacket. She whirls him around and says, "This is our last chance to make this right in granny's presence." She leans down into the casket with her face just a few inches from granny's body. Sobbing, she loudly wails, "Granny, I am so sorry for the hurt and rupture of our family." Grasped firmly by Marilyn's two hands, Bill is pulled into the casket as well. At first, he remains silent, but soon he too is sobbing and saying, "I am sorry, so sorry." After a few moments, the pastoral counselor is startled by Bill's standing straight up and running out of the church.

Seeking to understand this extraordinary situation, the pastoral counselor later speaks to both Bill and Marilyn. He asks Bill why he ran out of the church, and Bill responds, "There I was with my head just a few inches above granny's face and saying I was sorry. I opened my eyes and saw a smile on granny's face. I was so scared I ran out of the church." The pastoral counselor asks Marilyn how she feels about what just happened. She responds, "Just hearing Bill say he was sorry is enough for me. I never thought I would hear him say that. I have wanted to forgive him and now I have." After speaking to both Marilyn and Bill, the pastoral counselor realizes that the God of surprises has transformed a sabotaged forgiveness exchange into a successful forgiveness exchange.

The characters in this story fulfill their responsibilities in the forgiveness exchange. Marilyn confronts Bill and at the appropriate time transfers him to God, who increases the pressure on Bill until he is ready to repent. Marilyn is open to the workings of God in Bill's life and courageously seizes the opportunity God provides for them at the casket of their deceased grandmother. Bill repents and Marilyn extends the forgiveness she longed to extend for so many years. Bill receives the repentance, and the forgiveness exchange is complete.

> *"I am free! At long last, I am free!"*

In this exchange, the role of the pastoral counselor who did not condemn Marilyn to hell but responsibly led her through the steps of the forgiveness exchange should not be overlooked. In contrast to her pastor who presented Marilyn only with the option of forgiving and forgetting, this pastoral counselor became an occasion of grace for Marilyn and Bill and an instrument of God through the exercise of compassionate and competent ministry. As the characters in this story fulfill their responsibilities, God's grace far transcends all human expectations in their lives.

THE STALLED FORGIVENESS EXCHANGE:
HOPE AGAINST HOPE

The stalemate between Marge and her daughter continued, and Marge's circle of alienation widened. Other members of the family responsible for meeting Marge's increasing needs met to discuss her emotional and physical weakening. The meeting was an honest sharing about the impasse between Marge and Susan that the garage episode had precipitated, and the impact this relational rift had had on everyone over the span of numerous years. Both Marge's son Charles and the other daughter Maureen were able to find the words to talk about their mother's depression and its impact on their lives. Their children were able to acknowledge that they were aware of Grandma's depression and that they also struggled with knowing how to attend to her needs amid the demands of their own family and professional lives. The family agreed that it was time for Mom/Grandma to face the reality that she needed to explore a new, safer, and more adequate living situation.

Charles and Maureen made arrangements to visit with their mother to tell her about both the recent meeting and the family's encouragement that she needed another living option more responsive to her needs. Even though Marge was not forewarned, the visit appeared to go quite well, and Marge even willingly went with them to see the nearby retirement village. Marge expressed agreement to make the move, and Charles and Maureen assured their mother that they would handle all the details.

By the following morning, however, Marge had changed her mind and even saw the previous day as a plot by her children to take charge of her life against her will. As with the episode with Susan and Jack, Marge believed that she had become an unwitting victim of those seeking to take advantage of her. She raised suspicion about Maureen and Charles's motivation by speaking to Maureen's eldest daughter about their "taking her by surprise" and "the conspiratorial meeting against her." As with Susan, Maureen and Charles were stunned and deeply hurt by their mother's contention that they were the cause of her continuing isolation and suffering by their refusal to meet her desire to stay in her own home. Convinced that her own children have failed her, Marge will no longer telephone any of her children. She adamantly asserts, "If they want to know how I am doing, they can call me." The adult grandchildren remain confused and uncomfortable about how to proceed with their reactions to Grandma.

Susan, Maureen, and Charles are nearing the point of accepting that there may never be a resolution to their mother's unfinished business, a gesture of repentance toward Susan and Jack, or the restoration of the flow of love and trust between their mother and her three children. While holding onto the faith conviction of the power of grace and freedom and its unexpected and unanticipated manifestations, they abide, as we all do, within a human condition stamped by finitude and fallenness. Not everyone chooses to repent or develop the virtues for finishing unfinished business. Marge's patterns of refusal to accept responsibility for making the decisions that affect her well-being are deeply entrenched. While capable of being transformed by God's grace, she most probably will remain fixed by her insistence that others are more responsible than she for her life condition.

> *The challenge is to respect her freedom to live the consequences of her choices while not abandoning her.*

Allowing Marge to live the consequences of her free choices is terribly difficult and riddled with moments of guilt and confusion for her family. While her chronic depression and narcissistic tendencies remain untreated and unattended and are doubtless a source of her manipulative style, Marge remains an intellectually astute and resourceful person. Because Marge is narcissistic, she fails to grasp that the members of her family are real persons with their own hopes, dreams, and aspirations who need and expect something from her. For the narcissist, family members sadly become the "furniture of existence."[1] In a sense, the family is valued only in terms of how members perform for the narcissist, never in terms of who they are or what they mean in and of themselves.

The challenge for Marge's daughters and son is to respect her freedom to live the consequences of her choices while not abandoning her when those choices fail to bring relief to her misery. The lack of mutuality in the history of her relationships and the inability or refusal to engage in the art form of balancing the emotional ledgers in family life present those who love Marge with the challenge of both attending to her and simultaneously letting go. The impasse in the flow of love and trust begun with the rupture between Marge and Susan has now affected the entire family system. They cannot seem to overcome the patterns of estrangement. After the passage of so much time, the "stalled" or immobile relational plateau begins to deteriorate. As the hope for a change of understanding and attitude fades, the desire to be released from the burden of negotiating the pain emerges more powerfully. Thus, the option of the transfer of responsibility to God emerges as a realistic and realizable action for this family.

The breakthrough for this family may not be found in anticipating a change in Marge's perceptions or behavior or any further orchestrated interventions or confrontations on their part. Charles, Maureen, and Susan had hoped they would be the "places" of reconciliation and restoration for and with their mother. They now must trust, in freedom and grace, the reality of an active and healing God who works through the unexpected. They must transfer their mother to God. Each in his or her own way chooses to make this emotional and spiritual gesture.

Shortly after the transfer, Marge grew more distant, angry, and desperate and called Maureen to say, "I need to see you immediately . . . I am sick and so are you . . . you must come over immediately." Maureen was upset by the call but assured her that she would come to her home sometime that evening. Maureen called her therapist for advice and decided that she should not go alone to her mother's house. With hesitation, Maureen invited Charles to accompany her.

> *They must transfer their mother to God.*

Concerned and anxious, Charles and Maureen approached their mother's home. Marge appeared depressed but in reasonably good health. Nothing was said about the urgent call to Maureen, and the whole conversation focused on Marge's loneliness and her need for more visits from her family. Maureen and Charles received the information and after an hour indicated that they both had to be at work the following day and needed to leave. Maureen made a move to kiss her mother good-bye and Marge, sobbing, reached for her hand and expressed remorse about how hard it had been for Maureen in carrying so much of the burden that Marge has been over the years. Marge also reached out for Charles and expressed her concern for him.

The moment was unexpected and somewhat stunned Maureen and Charles. They embraced their mother and reaffirmed their love for her. Maureen had the presence of mind to tell her mother that she needed her to make efforts to express interest in her beyond what her mother needed from her. Maureen was holding her mother accountable and explaining how her mother could demonstrate her repentance. Maureen told her mother the whole family had been wounded by the stalemate between her and Susan. She begged her mother to seize the moment of empathy with humility and largesse of mind and heart and to reach out and break the silence between herself and Susan.

A Christian theology of repentance and forgiveness is incarnational—the word is embodied; the word is enacted and reveals the truth of the word spoken. The word of repentance is validated by the action that follows the offering of an apology. One knows that *new time* has dawned when new relational patterns replace hurtful behaviors. Grace transforms a moment in time to *kairos* but also sets the stage for a living out of the word of apology, regret, and spoken desire to repair the damage.

Marge did call Susan but initiated a conversation as if nothing had happened between them. Marge asked Susan to call her. Susan called the following weekend yet experienced no movement on her mother's part for authentic dialogue. Susan sensed her mother's pressure to resume the telephone exchange but not to initiate a forgiveness exchange. Marge and Susan have not talked to each other since. Marge did call her other daughter, Maureen, twice after her expression of contrition, but only in relation to the need for a ride to the doctor and to express her insistence that she be taken out one day.

While recent literature in life-span development suggests that the elderly are more likely to forgive than younger adults and have greater capacity for largesse, Marge remains committed to her vision of herself as deserving more love and care than she currently receives and as very much a hapless victim.[2] Years after the watershed fracture, the chasm between Marge and Susan has widened to engulf Maureen, Charles, and their respective families. Marge's refusal to truly repent and own her part in the fracture has resulted in her alienation from the family she so desperately desires.

> *New time has dawned when new relational patterns replace hurtful behaviors.*

Unfinished business for Marge remains unfinished. While the possibility of intra- and interpersonal change in Marge will exist until her death because of the pervasive reality of grace and her essential freedom to choose, she may indeed draw closure on her life without the healing resolutions longed for by those who love her. Elisabeth Kübler-Ross maintains that most people will die in character. What appeared to begin with an empty garage now symbolizes the emptiness of the whole of Marge's life. Narcissism clearly stunts the capacity for the giving and receiving of authentic love.[3] Marge's children will continue to attend to the challenges facing them in doing their emotional and spiritual homework and resist a complete severing of an empathic bond with their mother during the final season of her life's journey. The family's transfer of Marge to God, who is able to do abundantly more than anyone can ask or imagine, is this family's *special kind of hope* for their mother.

THE SUCCESSFUL FORGIVENESS EXCHANGE: CAN YOU DRINK THE CUP?[4]

Joseph Bernardin and well-respected Dutch pastoral theologian Henri Nouwen were good friends for more than twenty-five years.[5] Unexpectedly, Fr. Nouwen died just three months before Bernardin in 1996. Nouwen's last published work, *Can You Drink the Cup?*, was released a month before his death. It was this book that Joseph

Bernardin gave to some of his close associates and friends during the final months of his own life.[6] Can you drink the cup? was the question he was embracing and inviting others to embrace as well.

> "*The mother of the sons of Zebedee approached Jesus and said, 'Command that these two sons of mine sit, one at your right and the other at your left, in your kingdom.' Jesus replied, 'You do not know what you are asking. Can you drink the cup that I am going to drink?'" (Matt. 20:20–23)*

Bernardin's desire to shepherd God's people to the end impelled him to record his final journey in the phenomenally successful personal reflection he entitled *The Gift of Peace*. In his own words, Bernardin explores the painful cup of the false accusation that was his utter humiliation and triumph of character and courage. In Bernardin we see the virtues of the forgiving personality manifested as an art form of living, living well, and living to the end. Empathy, humility, gratitude, and largesse of mind and heart were endemic to Bernardin's pastoral spirituality. His commitment to prayer and a kind of praying that embraced life in the raw enabled God to work in and with him in the ministry of reconciliation. The exemplary administrator Bernardin became the shepherd Joseph.

Bernardin's encounter with his accuser, Steven Cook, in Philadelphia resulted in a successful forgiveness exchange. The confrontation by Bernardin was direct, and Cook's repentance was sincere and accepted. A reconciliation emerged that enabled both to remain in concerned relationship for the remainder of Steven's life. Interestingly, Bernardin records that Steven planned to visit him a few months after the reconciliation. Steven became too ill, however, and died at his mother's home on September 22, 1995, fully reconciled with the church. "'This,' he said, smiling from his deathbed at his mother about his return to the sacraments, 'is my gift to you.'"[7] Hence, the title Bernardin chose for his own final written words.

Steven's and Joseph's facing into the truth of the hurt and humiliation in the company of trusted others is testimony to the social and communal dimension of interpersonal wounding and healing. The

graced afternoon of their reconciliation included the celebration of
the sacraments of the Eucharist and the Anointing of the Sick. In *The
Gift of Peace*, the cardinal records his own words at the conclusion of
the liturgy that afternoon:

> In every family there are times when there is hurt, anger, or alienation.
> But we cannot run away from our family. We have only one family and
> so, after every falling out, we must make every effort to be reconciled.
> So, too, the Church is our spiritual family. Once we become a member,
> we may be hurt or become alienated, but it is still our family. Since
> there is no other, we must work at reconciliation. And that is what we
> have been doing this very afternoon.[8]

Their "afternoon of grace" can be seen as a metaphor for the deeply
human yearning for authentic peace in our relationships of meaning
and consequence. A successfully negotiated forgiveness exchange
inevitably results in the experience of confession and celebration that
brings the relationship into new time. The new time is the context in
which interpersonal reconciliation emerges, which always has social
and familial ramifications and implications. Simply said, peace shared
breeds peace. Love engendered gives birth to more love.

There is no way to seriously, faithfully, and gratefully negotiate the
challenges of "family" without the embrace of the question placed on
the lips of Jesus, who asked "Can you drink the cup I must drink?"
The Jesus of the Gospels understood that the cup of sorrow and the
cup of joy are the same cup. When we refuse to drink our cup in an
attempt to push aside the obligations and entitlements of the relationality to which we are called in love, "our lives become inauthen-
tic, insincere, superficial, and boring."[9] We can discover through
engaging the hard and hopeful work of healing the fractures between
and among us that the cup of rupture and reconciliation is the cup of
salvation. Nouwen says, "Drinking our cup is not simply adapting
ourselves to a bad situation and trying to use it as well as we can.
Drinking our cup is a hopeful, courageous, and self-confident *way of
living*" [italics ours].[10]

> *In Bernardin we see the virtues of the forgiving personal-
> ity manifested as an art form of living, living well, and liv-
> ing to the end.*

It is no surprise yet powerfully poignant that Joseph Bernardin chose to give Nouwen's book as a parting gift. Like Jesus and our brother Joseph, we agonize over the possibility that the cup could be taken from us. Is there anyone who has lived the journey of a life without Gethsemanes and seasons of abandonment and loneliness? So often these painful feelings are the felt consequences of the fractured bonds of love and trust in our relationships of meaning and consequence. So often the successful forgiveness exchange is sabotaged or stalled. The afternoon of grace awaits all who strive, albeit hesitatingly at times, to answer Jesus' question as a way of living.

APPLICATION

♦ From a biblical and spiritual point of view, the cup of blessing is the cup of sorrow. This is a paradox of faith. The cup of pain is the cup of promise; the cup of emptiness is the cup of fullness; the cup of suffering is the cup of salvation. What is the cup you are holding?

♦ Return to the story you have brought into the meaning and mystery of these pages, and through a journal entry enter an interior dialogue with the one with whom you seek repentance, forgiveness, and reconciliation. If you have done all you can do to restore your fractured relationship and have transferred the responsibility of accountability and forgiveness to God, leave your fractured relationship in the hands of God and trust God to eventually bring your relationship to resolution in God's own time. Create the conversation as you wish it to be in your "afternoon of grace."

NOTES

1. Theodore Millon and Roger Davis, *Personality Disorders in Modern Life* (New York: John Wiley and Sons, 2000), 289–308.

2. Ibid., 307.

3. Ibid., 290.

4. This particular successful forgiveness exchange resulted in a reconciliation, but not all successful forgiveness exchanges do. See chapter 2, pp. 14–15.

5. Joseph Cardinal Bernardin, *The Gift of Peace* (Chicago: Loyola University Press, 1997), 127.

6. Sister Brian Costello, R.S.M., chief of staff to Cardinal Bernardin, shared this information with Avis Clendenen in a conversation on July 10, 2000.

7. Bernardin, *Gift of Peace,* 41.

8. Ibid., 40.

9. Henri Nouwen, *Can You Drink the Cup?* (Notre Dame, Ind.: Ave Maria Press, 1996), 83.

10. Ibid., 82.

Bibliography

ᔌ

Alken, Martha. *The Healing Power of Forgiving*. New York: Crossroad, 1997.

Allen, Prudence. *The Concept of Woman: The Aristotelian Revolution, 750BC–1250AD*. Montreal: Eden Press, 1985.

Arnold, Johann Christoph. *Seventy Times Seven: The Power of Forgiveness*. Farmington, Pa.: Plough Publishing House, 1977.

Augsburger, David. *Caring Enough to Confront*. Ventura, Calif.: Regal Books, 1981.

———. *Caring Enough to Forgive: True and False Forgiveness*. Scottdale, Pa.: Herald Press, 1981.

———. *The Freedom of Forgiveness: 70 x 7*. Chicago: Moody, 1970.

———. *Helping People Forgive*. Louisville: Westminster John Knox, 1996.

Bass, Dorothy, ed. *Practicing Our Faith*. San Francisco: Jossey-Bass, 1997.

Beinert, Wolfgang, and Francis Schüssler-Fiorenza, eds. *Handbook of Catholic Theology*. New York: Crossroad, 1995.

Benner, David G., and Peter C. Hill, eds. *Baker Encyclopedia of Psychology and Counseling*. Grand Rapids: Baker, 1999.

Bernardin, Joseph Cardinal. *The Gift of Peace*. Chicago: Loyola University Press, 1997.

Betz, H. D. *The Sermon on the Mount: A Commentary on the Sermon on the Mount including the Sermon on the Plain (Matthew 5:3-7:27 and Luke 6:20-49)*. Hermeneia. Minneapolis: Fortress, 1995.

Bok, Sissela. *Lying: Moral Choice in Public and Private Life*. New York: Pantheon, 1978.

Boszormenyi-Nagi, I., and B. Krasner. *Between Give and Take: A Clinical Guide to Contextual Therapy*. New York: Brunner/Mazel, 1986.

————, and D. N. Ulrich. "Contextual Family Therapy." In *Handbook for Family Therapy*, edited by A. S. Gurman and D. P. Kniskern, 159–86. New York: Brunner/Mazel, 1981.

————, and G. Spark. *Invisible Partners*. New York: Brunner/Mazel, 1984.

Brakenhielm, Carl Reinhold. *Forgiveness*. Minneapolis: Fortress, 1993.

Brizee, Robert. *Eight Paths to Forgiveness*. St. Louis: Chalice, 1998.

Countryman, L. William. *Forgiven and Forgiving*. Harrisburg, Pa.: Morehouse Publishing, 1998.

Donnelly, Doris. *Learning to Forgive*. Nashville: Abingdon, 1979.

Egan, Harvey, trans. *Karl Rahner: I Remember*. New York: Crossroad, 1985.

Emmons, Robert A. "Is Spirituality an Intelligence? Motivation, Cognition, and the Psychology of Ultimate Concerns." *International Journal for the Psychology of Religion*, forthcoming.

————. "Personality and Forgiveness." In *Forgiveness: Theory, Research, and Practice*, edited by Michael E. McCullough, Kenneth I. Pargament, and Carl E. Thoresen, 156–75. New York: Guilford Press, 2000.

Enright, Robert, Elizabeth A. Gassin, and Ching-Ru Wu. "Forgiveness: A Developmental View." *Journal of Moral Education* 21, no. 2 (1992): 99–114.

————, and The Human Development Study Group. "The Moral Development of Forgiveness." In *Moral Behavior and Development*, vol. 1, edited by W. Kurtiness and J. Gewirtz, 23–152. Hillsdale, N.J.: Erlbaum, 1991.

————, and Joanna North, eds. *Exploring Forgiveness*. Madison: University of Wisconsin Press, 1998.

Erikson, Erik. *Childhood and Society*. New York: W. W. Norton, 1950.

————. *Identity and the Life Cycle*. New York: W. W. Norton, 1980.

Fackre, Gabriel, ed. *Judgment Day at the White House: A Critical Declaration Exploring Moral Issues and the Political Use and Abuse of Religion*. Grand Rapids: Eerdmans, 1999.

Flanagan, Beverly. *Forgiving the Unforgivable*. New York: Macmillan, 1992.

Floristan, Casiano, and Christian Duquoc, eds. *Forgiveness*. Edinburgh: T. & T. Clark, 1986.

Fowler, James W. *Becoming Adult, Becoming Christian*. San Francisco: Harper & Row, 1984.

Gestrich, Christof. *The Return of Splendor in the World: The Christian Doctrine of Sin and Forgiveness*. Grand Rapids: Eerdmans, 1997.

Hargrave, Terry. *Families and Forgiveness: Healing Wounds in the Intergenerational Family*. New York: Brunner/Mazel Publishers, 1994.

————, and William Anderson. *Finishing Well: Aging and Reparation in the Intergenerational Family*. New York: Brunner/Mazel Publishers, 1992.

————, and Suzanne Midori Hanna, eds. *The Aging Family: New Visions in Theory, Practice, and Reality*. New York: Brunner/Mazel Publishers, 1997.

Harrison, Beverly Wildung. "The Power of Anger in the Work of Love." In *Weaving the Vision*, edited by Judith Plaskow and Carol Christ, 214–25. San Francisco: Harper & Row, 1989.

Hellwig, Monika. *What Are the Theologians Saying Now?* Westminster, Md.: Christian Classics, 1992.

Herman, Judith L. *Trauma and Recovery*. New York: Basic Books, 1992.

Hyde, Clark. *To Declare God's Forgiveness: Toward a Pastoral Theology of Reconciliation*. Wilton, Conn.: Morehouse Barlow Co., 1984.

Imhof, Paul, and Hubert Baillowons, eds. *Karl Rahner in Dialogue: Conversations and Interviews, 1965–1982*. New York: Crossroad, 1986.

Jegen, Carol Frances. *Restoring Our Friendship with God: The Mystery of Redemption from Suffering and Sin*. Wilmington, Del.: Michael Glazier, 1989.

Johnson, Robert. *Owning Your Own Shadow: Understanding the Dark Side of the Psyche*. San Francisco: Harper, 1991.

Jones, L. Gregory. *Embodying Forgiveness: A Theological Analysis*. Grand Rapids: Eerdmans, 1995.

Koenig, Harold. *The Healing Power of Faith*. New York: Simon & Schuster, 1999.

————. *Religion and Health*. New York: Oxford University Press, 2000.

Kopas, Jane. *Sacred Identity: Exploring a Theology of the Person*. New York: Paulist, 1994.

Kübler-Ross, Elisabeth. *Death Is of Vital Importance*. Barrytown, N.Y.: Station Hill Press, 1995.

————. *On Life after Death*. Berkeley, Calif.: Celestial Arts, 1991.

Lambert, Jean Christine. *The Human Action of Forgiving*. Lanham, Md.: University Press of America, 1985.

Lehmann, Karl, and Albert Raffelt, eds. *Karl Rahner: The Content of Faith*. New York: Crossroad, 1994.

Linn, Dennis, Sheila Fabricant Linn, and Matthew Linn. *Don't Forgive Too Soon: Extending the 2 Hands that Heal*. New York: Paulist, 1997.

Linn, Dennis, and Matthew Linn. *Healing Life's Hurts: Healing Memories Through Five Stages of Forgiveness*. New York: Paulist, 1978.

Logue, Judy. *Forgiving the People You Love to Hate*. Ligouri, Mo.: Ligouri Press, 1997.

Malcolm, Wanda M., and Leslie S. Greenberg. "Forgiveness as Process of Change in Individual Psychotherapy." In *Forgiveness: Theory, Research, and Practice*, edited by Michael E. McCullough, Kenneth I. Pargament, and Carl E. Thoresen, 179–202. New York: Guilford Press, 2000.

McBrien, Richard. *Catholicism*. San Francisco: HarperCollins, 1994.

McCool, Gerald A., ed. *A Rahner Reader*. New York: Seabury Press, 1975.

McCullough, Michael E., Kenneth I. Pargament, and Carol E. Thoresen. *Forgiveness: Theory, Research, and Practice*. New York: Guilford Press, 2000.

————, Steven Sandage, and Everett Worthington. *To Forgive Is Human: How to Put Your Past in the Past*. Downers Grove, Ill.: InterVarsity, 1997.

Meninger, William A. *The Process of Forgiveness*. New York: Continuum, 1996.

Miller, Alice. *Breaking Down the Walls of Silence: The Liberating Experience of Facing Painful Truth*. New York: Penguin, 1991.

Millon, Theodore, and Roger Davis. *Personality Disorders in Modern Life*. New York: John Wiley and Sons, 2000.

Myers, David G. "Close Relationships and Quality of Life." In *Foundations of Hedonic Psychology: Scientific Perspectives on Enjoyment and Suffering*, edited by D. Kahnerman, E. Diener, and N.

Schwarz. New York: Russell Sage Foundation, forthcoming.

————. *The Pursuit of Happiness: Who Is Happy—and Why*. New York: Avon Press, 1992.

Nouwen, Henri. *Can You Drink the Cup?* Notre Dame: Ave Maria Press, 1996.

Patton, John. *Is Human Forgiveness Possible? A Pastoral Care Perspective*. Nashville: Abingdon, 1985.

Plaskow, Judith, and Carol Christ. *Weaving the Visions*. San Francisco: Harper & Row, 1989.

Rahner, Karl. *Foundations of Christian Faith*. New York: Crossroad, 1984.

————. *Theological Investigations: Penance in the Early Church*. Vol. 15. New York: Crossroad, 1982.

Raskin, R., and H. Terry. "A Principal Components Analysis of the Narcissistic Personality Inventory and Further Evidence of Its Construct Validity." *Journal of Personality and Social Psychology* 54 (1988): 890–902.

Sachs, John. *The Christian Vision of Humanity: Basic Christian Anthropology*. Collegeville, Minn.: Liturgical Press, 1991.

Schipperges, Heinrich. *Hildegard of Bingen: Healing and the Nature of the Cosmos*. Princeton: Markus Wiener Publishers, 1997.

Schreiter, Robert J. *The Ministry of Reconciliation: Spirituality and Strategies*. Maryknoll, N.Y.: Orbis, 1998.

Shriver, Donald W., Jr. *An Ethic for Enemies: Forgiveness in Politics*. New York: Oxford University Press, 1995.

Smedes, Louis B. *Forgive and Forget: Healing the Hurts We Didn't Deserve*. San Francisco: Harper & Row, 1984.

Sperry, L., and H. L. Ansbacher. "The Concept of Narcissism and Narcissistic Personality Disorder." In *Psychopathology and Psychotherapy*, edited by L. Sperry and J. Carlson, 337–51. Washington, D.C.: Accelerated Development, 1996.

Stanley, Charles. *Experiencing Forgiveness*. Nashville: Thomas Nelson, 1996.

Thomas, Gary. "The Forgiveness Factor." *Christianity Today* 44 (January 10, 2000): 38–51.

Whitehead, James D., and Evelyn Eaton Whitehead. *Shadows of the Heart: A Spirituality of the Painful Emotions*. New York: Crossroad, 1994.

Wink, Walter. *When the Powers Fall: Reconciliation in the Healing of Nations.* Minneapolis: Fortress Press, 1998.

Wogamon, Philip. *From the Eye of the Storm: A Pastor to the President Speaks Out.* Louisville: Westminster John Knox, 1998.

Wolman, Benjamin B., ed. *Dictionary of Behavioral Science.* New York: Van Nostrand Reinhold Company, 1973.

Worthington, Everett J., Jr. *Dimensions of Forgiveness: Psychological Research and Theological Perspectives.* Philadelphia: Templeton Foundation Press, 1998.